DETROIT PUBLIC LIBRARY

3 5674 03564503 6

D0858280

Jewel

DETROIT PUBLIC LIBRARY

CHANEY BRANCH LIBRARY
16101 GRAND RIVER
DETROIT, MI 48227

DATE DUE

OCT 0 1 2002

FEB 1 9 2003

APR 2 1 2003

FEB 2 4 2004

BC-3

AUG - - 2002

CY

ANGELA
BASSETT

ANGELA BASSETT

Dawn FitzGerald

CHELSEA HOUSE PUBLISHERS
Philadelphia

Chelsea House Publishers

Editor in Chief	Sally Cheney
Associate Editor in Chief	Kim Shinners
Production Manager	Pamela Loos
Art Director	Sara Davis
Cover Designer	Robert Gerson

© 2002 by Chelsea House Publishers, a subsidiary of Haights Cross
Communications. All rights reserved. Printed and bound in the United
States of America.

The Chelsea House World Wide Web address is
http://www.chelseahouse.com

Produced by Pre-Press Company, Inc.,
East Bridgewater, Mass.

First Printing
1 3 5 7 9 8 6 4 2

            Library of Congress Cataloging-in-Publication Data

FitzGerald, Dawn.
    Angela Bassett / Dawn FitzGerald.
        p. cm. — (Black Americans of achievement)
    Includes bibliographical references and index.
    ISBN 0-7910-5810-7 (alk. paper)— ISBN 0-7910-5811-5 (pbk. : alk. paper)
    1. Bassett, Angela—Juvenile literature. 2. Motion picture actors and
actresses—United States—Biography— Juvenile literature. 3. African
American motion picture actors and actresses—United States—Biography—
Juvenile literature. [1. Bassett, Angela. 2. Actors and actresses. 3. African
Americans—Biography. 4. Women—Biography.] I. Title. II. Series.

PN2287.B384 A3 2001
791.43'028'092—dc21
[B]   2001028799

*Angela Bassett has spent many
years honing her craft as an
actress. Today, she is well known
for her riveting performances and
captivating good looks.*

CONTENTS

BLACK AMERICANS OF ACHIEVEMENT

HENRY AARON
baseball great

KAREEM ABDUL-JABBAR
basketball great

MUHAMMAD ALI
heavyweight champion

RICHARD ALLEN
religious leader and social activist

MAYA ANGELOU
author

LOUIS ARMSTRONG
musician

ARTHUR ASHE
tennis great

JOSEPHINE BAKER
entertainer

JAMES BALDWIN
author

TYRA BANKS
model

BENJAMIN BANNEKER
scientist and mathematician

COUNT BASIE
bandleader and composer

ANGELA BASSETT
actress

ROMARE BEARDEN
artist

HALLE BERRY
actress

MARY MCLEOD BETHUNE
educator

GEORGE WASHINGTON
CARVER
botanist

JOHNNIE COCHRAN
lawyer

BILL COSBY
entertainer

MILES DAVIS
musician

FREDERICK DOUGLASS
abolitionist editor

CHARLES DREW
physician

W. E. B. DU BOIS
scholar and activist

PAUL LAURENCE DUNBAR
poet

DUKE ELLINGTON
bandleader and composer

RALPH ELLISON
author

JULIUS ERVING
basketball great

LOUIS FARRAKHAN
political activist

ELLA FITZGERALD
singer

ARETHA FRANKLIN
entertainer

MORGAN FREEMAN
actor

MARCUS GARVEY
black nationalist leader

JOSH GIBSON
baseball great

WHOOPI GOLDBERG
entertainer

CUBA GOODING JR.
actor

ALEX HALEY
author

PRINCE HALL
social reformer

JIMI HENDRIX
musician

MATTHEW HENSON
explorer

GREGORY HINES
performer

BILLIE HOLIDAY
singer

LENA HORNE
entertainer

WHITNEY HOUSTON
singer and actress

LANGSTON HUGHES
poet

JANET JACKSON
musician

JESSE JACKSON
civil-rights leader and politician

MICHAEL JACKSON
entertainer

SAMUEL L. JACKSON
actor

T. D. JAKES *religious leader*	RONALD MCNAIR *astronaut*	COLIN POWELL *military leader*	ALICE WALKER *author*
JACK JOHNSON *heavyweight champion*	MALCOLM X *militant black leader*	PAUL ROBESON *singer and actor*	MADAM C. J. WALKER *entrepreneur*
MAGIC JOHNSON *basketball great*	BOB MARLEY *musician*	JACKIE ROBINSON *baseball great*	BOOKER T. WASHINGTON *educator*
SCOTT JOPLIN *composer*	THURGOOD MARSHALL *Supreme Court justice*	CHRIS ROCK *comedian and actor*	DENZEL WASHINGTON *actor*
BARBARA JORDAN *politician*	TERRY MCMILLAN *author*	DIANA ROSS *entertainer*	J. C. WATTS *politician*
MICHAEL JORDAN *basketball great*	TONI MORRISON *author*	WILL SMITH *actor*	VANESSA WILLIAMS *singer and actress*
CORETTA SCOTT KING *civil-rights leader*	ELIJAH MUHAMMAD *religious leader*	WESLEY SNIPES *actor*	OPRAH WINFREY *entertainer*
MARTIN LUTHER KING, JR. *civil-rights leader*	EDDIE MURPHY *entertainer*	CLARENCE THOMAS *Supreme Court justice*	TIGER WOODS *golf star*
LEWIS LATIMER *scientist*	JESSE OWENS *champion athlete*	SOJOURNER TRUTH *antislavery activist*	RICHARD WRIGHT *author*
SPIKE LEE *filmmaker*	SATCHEL PAIGE *baseball great*	HARRIET TUBMAN *antislavery activist*	
CARL LEWIS *champion athlete*	CHARLIE PARKER *musician*	NAT TURNER *slave revolt leader*	
JOE LOUIS *heavyweight champion*	ROSA PARKS *civil-rights leader*	TINA TURNER *entertainer*	

ON
ACHIEVEMENT

***

Coretta Scott King

Before you begin this book, I hope you will ask yourself what the word *excellence* means to you. I think it's a question we should all ask, and keep asking as we grow older and change. Because the truest answer to it should never change. When you think of excellence, perhaps you think of success at work; or of becoming wealthy; or meeting the right person, getting married, and having a good family life.

Those goals are worth striving for, but there is a better way to look at excellence. As Martin Luther King Jr. said in one of his last sermons, "I want you to be first in love. I want you to be first in moral excellence. I want you to be first in generosity. If you want to be important, wonderful. If you want to be great, wonderful. But recognize that he who is greatest among you shall be your servant."

My husband knew that the true meaning of achievement is service. When I met him, in 1952, he was already ordained as a Baptist minister and was working toward a doctoral degree at Boston University. I was studying at the New England Conservatory and dreamed of accomplishments in music. We married a year later, and after I graduated the following year we moved to Montgomery, Alabama. We didn't know it then, but our notions of achievement were about to undergo a dramatic change.

You may have read or heard about what happened next. What began with the boycott of a local bus line grew into a national crusade, and by the time he was assassinated in 1968 my husband had fashioned a black movement powerful enough to shatter forever the practice of racial segregation. What you may not have read about is where he learned to resist injustice without compromising his religious beliefs.

He adopted a strategy of nonviolence from a man of a different race, who lived in a different country and even practiced a different religion. The man was Mahatma Gandhi, the great leader of India, who devoted his life to serving humanity in the spirit of love and nonviolence. It was in these principles that Martin discovered his method for social reform. More than anything else, those two principles were the key to his achievements.

These books are about African Americans who served society through the excellence of their achievements. They form part of the rich history of black men and women in America—a history of stunning accomplishments in every field of human endeavor, from literature and art to science, industry, education, diplomacy, athletics, jurisprudence, even polar exploration.

Not all of the people in this history had the same ideals, but I think you will find that all of them had something in common. Like Martin Luther King Jr., they all decided to become "drum majors" and serve humanity. In that principle—whether it was expressed in books, inventions, or song—they found a goal and a guide outside themselves that showed them a way to serve others instead of living only for themselves.

Reading the stories of these courageous men and women not only helps us discover the principles that we will use to guide our own lives; it also teaches us about our black heritage and about America itself. It is crucial for us to know the heroes and heroines of our history and to realize that the price we paid in our struggle for equality in America was dear. But we must also understand that we have gotten as far as we have partly because America's democratic system and ideals made it possible.

We are still struggling with racism and prejudice. But the great men and women in this series are a tribute to the spirit of the country in which they have flourished. And that makes their stories special and worth knowing.

1

THEY KNOW WHO I AM

❧

ANGELA BASSETT COULDN'T sleep. Tossing and turning, she kept checking the clock on her nightstand. It was only 3 A.M., and the morning seemed so far away.

For the rest of the world, the next day would be an ordinary one in February 1994. But for the people involved in the Hollywood film industry the day would bring either triumph or disappointment. Writers, directors, actors—anyone connected with making movies would anxiously wait for the Academy Award nominations to be announced.

Although not as exciting as Oscar night, when the golden statues are presented to the winners, the day that Academy Award nominations are announced is important in Hollywood. Being chosen as one of five nominees in a category is a high honor and a definite validation of talent. Angela hoped that the film that had changed her life would bring her a Best Actress nomination, announcing to Hollywood and the entire world that a star had been born.

As Angela showered and dressed that morning, she may have paused for a moment to look at her reflection in the bathroom mirror. She'd smile, remembering twenty years earlier when she had stood in front of a different bathroom mirror, a shy

Receiving an Oscar is one of the highest achievements in all of filmmaking. Angela's nomination for her performance in What's Love Got to Do with It? *was much-deserved recognition of her hard work.*

Audiences and critics were thrilled with Angela's performance as Tina Turner in What's Love Got to Do with It? *The praise Angela received for her role in the film finally made Hollywood take notice of her wide array of talents.*

15-year-old from the projects of St. Petersburg, Florida, practicing her lines for the high school play.

Angela would recall the thunderous applause of that first standing ovation she had received for her role as Mama in *A Raisin in the Sun*. Twenty years later, would her high-voltage performance as rock and roll legend Tina Turner in *What's Love Got to Do with It?* bring the 35-year-old actress the recognition she had worked for her entire adult life?

Critics said the movie had been released too early in the summer to attract serious consideration for the Oscar nominations. They said Bassett was a relative unknown in the Hollywood film industry. It was not until after the movie had been released that director Steven Spielberg asked her, "Where have you been?"

Angela knew the answer to that question. Right here in Hollywood, working hard all along. In the process, she had developed a reputation for transforming supporting roles and bit parts into performances that glowed with the intensity of her honest portrayals. She was known as a hardworking actress: patient and persistent.

But on this day, patience was hard to come by. Angela had given her all to *What's Love Got to Do with It?* A dialect coach, a singing coach, a choreographer, and a personal trainer had helped prepare her to play the incomparable Tina Turner. In order to look more like Tina, Angela had lifted weights for two hours a day, six days a week. She drank over a gallon of water daily and went on a high protein, no-sweets diet—egg whites, tuna without mayo, and vegetables. Angela had just one month before shooting began to obtain Tina's muscular physique and to learn songs and dance routines.

Two hours before the Oscar nominations were to be announced, a jittery Angela Bassett drove over to her friend Wren Brown's house. Good news or bad, she wanted to share the moment with someone who knew her well.

As she drove along the Los Angeles highway, Angela may have reflected on how few African-American women have been nominated for Best Actress. In 1954, Dorothy Dandridge was nominated for her role in *Carmen*. In the 1970s, Cicely Tyson, Diana Ross, and Diahann Carroll received Best Actress nominations. In 1985, Whoopi Goldberg received a Best Actress nomination for *The Color Purple*. But none of these actresses won the Oscar.

Hattie McDaniel, who played Mammy in the 1939 film *Gone with the Wind*, actually won the Oscar for Best Supporting Actress. McDaniel was the first black to win an Academy Award. In 1990 Whoopi Goldberg also won an Oscar for Best Supporting Actress for the movie *Ghost*. In the 73-year history of the Academy Awards, only two black actresses had won for supporting roles. No black actress had won an Oscar in the Best Actress category and the previous nomination received by Whoopie Goldberg was ten years prior.

Laurence Fishburne and Angela Bassett, cast as Ike and Tina Turner, respectively, received recognition for their work in What's Love Got to Do With It? *Both actors were nominated for an Oscar.*

Angela and Wren sat in front of the television, eyes riveted to the screen. "The Oscar nominations were announced today by the Academy of Motion Picture Arts and Sciences," said the reporter on the five o'clock news. "For the category of Best Actor, the nominees are Daniel Day-Lewis, *In the Name of the Father*; Tom Hanks, *Philadelphia*; Anthony Hopkins, *The Remains of the Day*; Liam Neeson, *Schindler's List*; and Laurence Fishburne, *What's Love Got to Do with It?*"

Angela shot off the couch, "Yes!" She and Laurence Fishburne had been good friends for many years. They had worked together in the movies *Boyz N the Hood* and *What's Love Got to Do with It?* Angela was thrilled that Laurence was nominated. If Laurence had received a nomination, the Academy had at least noticed the film. Now, the question was, had they noticed Angela?

The reporter continued, "In the Best Actress category the nominees are . . ."

Angela glanced at Wren, whose fingers, arms, and legs were crossed.

"Stockard Channing, *Six Degrees of Separation*; Holly Hunter, *The Piano*; Emma Thompson, *The Remains of the Day*; Debra Winger, *Shadowlands*; and Angela Bassett, *What's Love Got to Do with It?*"

Angela jumped off the couch for the second time that day, "They know who I am!" she cried. "They know who I am!"

2

FROM HARLEM TO
NEW HAVEN

— ❧ —

Angela's life today, surrounded by the glamour of Hollywood, is far different than the one she knew as a child. Times were often difficult for the Bassett family as Angela's mother struggled to raise her children on her own.

Angela Bassett was born in Harlem in New York City on August 16, 1958. In the 1950s and 1960s Harlem was a turbulent place. Malcolm X had arrived to head the Harlem Mosque and created an independent religious and Black Nationalist movement that declared themselves ready to fight. Half of all housing units in Harlem were unsound, and the infant mortality rate was nearly double that of the rest of the city. In the early 1960s, an off-duty police officer shot a black youth and rioting began. Two people were killed and hundreds injured. Stores were looted for several days.

Times were tough in the Bassett household. Angela's father had abandoned the family. In 1962, after divorcing her husband, Angela's mother, Betty Bassett, moved Angela and her sister D'nette, who was 14 months younger, to St. Petersburg, Florida, in hopes of finding a better life for her children. Unfortunately, the projects of St. Petersburg were not much better than the projects of Harlem. "I grew up in a place where people were selling drugs down the hall," Angela has recalled. "My childhood was filled with wondering if our apartment would be broken into when I got home."

Despite the rough neighborhood, Betty Bassett worked hard and provided a loving and stable home life for her children. Angela's aunt helped take care of the girls while Betty worked a full-time job

In an attempt to give her children a better environment to grow in, Betty Bassett moved the family from the sometimes cruel streets of Harlem to the city of St. Petersburg, Florida.

during the day and attended night school to improve her skills. She eventually landed a job working for the Florida Welfare Department as a social worker. Betty taught Angela important life lessons by setting an independent, hard-working example. "Get it for yourself, Angela! Betty urged her daughter. "Get your own so you don't have to rely on anyone else!"

Betty certainly refused to rely on any man. She remarried in the hopes of providing a father for her two growing daughters. According to Angela, the marriage was extremely brief—one week. Betty had too much self-respect to tolerate any abuse. "She immediately annulled the marriage," recalls Angela. "After seven days—boom!—annulled. That's my example. You don't have to suffer in silence."

Angela's mother set high expectations for her children academically. From an early age Angela knew she would be going to college. "My mother stayed on our tails," Bassett told the *New York Daily News*. "With my mother, you just knew for years and years and years you were going to college. There was no alternative." Angela worked hard at Boca Ciega High School, outside St. Petersburg, to achieve this goal.

Angela's favorite subject in school was British literature. For a future actress, it wasn't surprising that she enjoyed reading Shakespeare. She vividly remembers reading aloud *Romeo and Juliet* for the first time. When her teacher assigned parts for the play, Angela eagerly volunteered. She loved the language, the passion, and the story.

Angela was the first black student invited to join the National Honor Society at Boca Ciega High School. She was a popular student who participated in cheerleading and student government. Surprisingly, for an actress known for her physical strength and muscular beauty, there was one class in school that Angela dreaded taking—physical education. "Phys ed was my worst subject in school," Angela told *Newsday*. "My classmates would say, 'Oh, she never wants to play fair.' No! I didn't! Not if I couldn't win!"

Angela's teachers and guidance counselors noticed Angela's competitive spirit and drive to succeed. They recommended her for Upward Bound, a federally funded program designed to help motivated and talented students from low-income families pursue a college education. Students in Upward Bound participate in intensive six-week summer programs held on a college campus. They also receive academic and support services during the school year, typically on weekends or after school.

Angela's involvement with Upward Bound provided her first exposure to the theater. When she was 15, Angela was chosen to represent her school at an

James Earl Jones was an inspiration to Angela. When she saw him in a performance of the play Of Mice and Men, *she knew from then on that she wanted to make acting a significant part of her life.*

Upward Bound conference in Washington, D.C. It was there that she saw James Earl Jones perform in John Steinbeck's *Of Mice and Men* at the Kennedy Center. Jones played Lenny in the heartbreaking story of two wanderers who care for each other in their desperate search for a home of their own. Angela said of the performance, "It was so pure, so honest. I cried my eyes out."

Jones's passionate performance forged a lifetime commitment in Angela to want to act. She realized that "an honest portrayal can provoke an audience. Right then I decided, I want to do that." Angela returned from her Washington trip and immediately began working toward her goal, taking on roles in school plays and community theater productions.

At Boca Ciega High School Angela enrolled in the drama club. The program at that time wasn't a very extensive one, but Angela and the other students made the best of it. For a shy, young girl, playing the role of Mama in Lorraine Hansbury's *A Raisin in the Sun* gave Angela confidence and helped her find her voice. Speaking the monologues of her part in front of an audience was challenging. At the end of the show, when she received a standing ovation, Angela said she felt "shocked, afraid, and encouraged!"

Meanwhile, Angela's mother continued to monitor her daughter's progress in school. There were strict consequences if Betty thought Angela wasn't working up to her abilities. Periodically, Betty would visit the school to find out how her daughter was doing. With all of Angela's teachers assembled for a conference, Betty would grill them on the teenager's academic progress. Angela told *USA Today*, "She'd be so hard that the teachers would come to my defense. 'Well, I really don't think you need to take Angela off cheerleading. . . .'"

But Betty had high expectations for her daughter and Angela did her best to fulfill them. She claims that the worst thing she ever did in school was to try to hitch a ride home one evening after choir practice. Walking along the side of the road, she and a girl-friend stuck their thumbs out but quickly pulled them back as a car approached. Eventually, they worked up the nerve to thumb a ride. The next car that passed pulled over to the side of the road and a familiar face leaned out the window. It was Angela's choir director.

After the hitchhiking incident was reported to her mother, Angela never dared try that again. Even at that age, Angela cared about her reputation and its impact on her dreams of becoming a famous actress. She explained, "I thought, I'd be in the public eye someday and didn't want people saying bad things about me."

Throughout the high school years, Betty encouraged Angela and her sister D'nette to stick together and support each other no matter what. When Angela was invited to parties, she had to take D'nette along with her. There were many times when D'nette would decide that she didn't like something at the party and she would begin to walk home alone. Whether Angela was ready to leave or not, she would remember her mother's advice to stay together and would wind up chasing D'nette down the street.

Studying, acting in school plays, sometimes talking with boys on the telephone, and dreaming about singing with the Jackson Five filled up Angela's days during her senior year of high school. The vice-principal at Boca Ciega High School and a local director of the Upward Bound program encouraged Angela to apply for a scholarship at Harvard or Yale University. With her excellent grades and her involvement in extracurricular activities, they believed that Angela had a chance of obtaining a scholarship to an elite college. Angela wasn't so sure, "I had no exposure beyond St. Petersburg. I didn't know about those options."

Despite such reservations, she decided to complete the rigorous application process for Yale University in New Haven, Connecticut. One of the top schools in the country, Yale receives over 13,000 applications every year, but accepts fewer than 1,400 students in the freshman class. Angela mailed her application and then began the long wait.

In mid-April, when college acceptance and rejection letters were being mailed to applicants, Angela practically camped out near her mailbox to wait for the news. The postman virtually became her new best friend. "I still remember getting the acceptance letter in the mail," Angela told USA Today. "My mother was jumping on the bed, ecstatic. I was all quiet thinking, I'm going to have to go there. All the smartest people in the world are there." Betty's dream for her children had come true.

In early autumn 1976, when Betty sent her first-born off to Yale, she reminded her to keep her grades up, maintain her focus, and stay true to her calling. Her parting words to Angela were, "Get an education, not a husband!"

Angela did just that. As she worked toward a bachelor's degree in African-American studies, Angela continued to excel academically. But in the beginning it wasn't easy for her to feel accepted in her new environment. She felt intimidated by all "those brainiacs from prep schools" who were now her classmates. But Angela remembered her mother's support and encouragement and chose to have faith in herself and her goals. Angela told the *Los Angeles Times*, "I did think that I should perhaps be more practical about my career and go to business school. But that thought lasted for maybe about a year. And it was in my junior year that I decided to give my dreams a shot."

In 1976 Angela began her first year at Yale University. After receiving her degree, Angela continued to follow her dream of being an actress and applied for entry into Yale's prestigious School of Drama.

Meryl Streep, seen here in the film One True Thing, *was one of many actresses who attended the Yale School of Drama. Angela hoped that the school would accept her and that she would finally be on the road to fulfilling her acting dreams.*

As an aspiring black actress, Angela realized the difficulty she was up against in finding work. "It didn't make sense for me to become an actress," she told the *Toronto Sun*, "There were so few role models for me on television or in film. It just didn't make sense because it just didn't seem like you could keep a roof over your head as a black actress."

Still, the determination that carried Angela from the projects of St. Petersburg to an Ivy League university required that she pursue her dream and apply to the Yale School of Drama, despite the slim prospects for a successful acting career. She reasoned that there would always be opportunities in New York City and in regional theaters if film and television roles were scarce.

The Yale School of Drama is one of the most prestigious drama schools in the country, having graduated such renowned actors as Meryl Streep, Sigourney Weaver, and Frances McDormand. The acting department of the school admits talented and committed individuals who possess intelligence, a strong imagination, and physical and vocal talents capable of development. The school prepares its students for work as professional actors by combining in-depth classroom training with extensive production work. After three years of rigorous study and training, students graduate with a Master of Fine Arts. Although Angela could have applied to many other drama schools in the country, she decided to apply only to Yale.

Angela auditioned for acceptance to the school by performing a selection from one of Shakespeare's plays. She was also required to present a four-minute selection from a modern prose piece before a panel of judges. Thousands of auditions for the Yale School of Drama take place in Chicago, San Francisco, and New Haven every year. Angela hoped that once again she would be one of the lucky few to receive the coveted acceptance letter.

Angela wasn't disappointed. After four years of undergraduate work at Yale, she would finally have the opportunity to study what had been her first love since she was 15 years old—acting. More importantly, Angela would learn the craft of acting under the celebrated Broadway director Lloyd Richards who was the director of the Yale School of Drama at that time.

Richards had a tremendous impact on Angela's acting technique. "Lloyd Richards was incredible," Angela told *Essence*. "He insisted that I be honest in the work, even if it was painful. He always told me, 'The audience doesn't want to see how hard you're working. Make it look honest and effortless.'"

Angela recalls Richards telling his students, "Don't wave the rubber chicken!" At first puzzled by this expression, Angela quickly learned what it meant: Don't reveal too much to the audience when you're acting; let the audience do some of the work.

Making acting look effortless became Angela's goal. "The mark of a true professional," according to

The famous Broadway director Lloyd Richards was one of Angela's professors at the Yale School of Drama.

Angela, "is being able to get up and do it, even though it's hard work, but you don't make it look like it's hard work." The discipline she learned from Richards at Yale combined with the work ethic she learned from her mother would become the core values on which Angela would build her professional career.

But no one said it would be easy. One of the most challenging classes during her three years at Yale Drama was the required first-year movement class. A month before school began, Angela had to undergo surgery on the base of her spine. During her slow and painful recovery, she somehow managed to complete a class devoted to teaching not only dance basics but all movement associated with stage acting—which included pretending to be punched, slapped, stabbed, shoved, and thrown to the ground. Quitting was never an option. Needless to say, the girl who disliked physical education in high school somehow found the strength to survive first-year movement.

One of the highlights of Angela's years at Yale School of Drama was a visit from the man who had inspired her with his performance in *Of Mice and Men* ten years earlier. James Earl Jones came to do a play with Angela's class. Angela had the rare opportunity to tell her idol that he was the reason she had chosen to pursue an acting career.

An actor of incredible range—who has mastered roles from Shakespeare to *Star Wars*—Jones taught Angela's class many things about acting during his visit. Most important was the idea that acting should be brave, that it should transcend everyday life and reveal universal truths about human existence.

Listening to Jones at that time, Angela didn't know that she would soon need all the bravery and tenacity her spirit could gather for the next challenge in her life. She was about to graduate from a prestigious school of acting and try to make a name for herself in the indifferent New York theater world. Angela was more than ready to launch her career. Was New York ready for Angela?

3

PAYING HER DUES

◀◉▶

After graduating from the Yale
School of Drama, Angela was
well on her way to beginning
her career as an actress. There
were still plenty of hurdles for
Angela to overcome, but she
was prepared to meet them
head on.

AFTER GRADUATING FROM the Yale
School of Drama in 1983, Angela moved into a studio apartment at 105th Street and Central Park West
in Manhattan. During the day, she worked as a receptionist in a beauty salon; at night, she practiced
monologues in her bathroom mirror trying to keep
her acting skills sharp. Booking manicures and hair-
cutting appointments was not how Angela envi-
sioned using her Yale degrees, but she hoped the job
would offer her some flexibility to go out on auditions. Angela recalls, "The people there just didn't
understand the job was only a means to the end and
coming back late from lunch was the price of making
it to auditions."

Not surprisingly, Angela's job as a receptionist
didn't last long. She next took a job with *U.S. News
and World Report* as a photo researcher and continued
to audition for parts in Broadway, off-Broadway, and
off-off-Broadway plays. Like many actors beginning
their careers, Angela got her first break in an off-off-
Broadway production. After ten months of unsuc-
cessful auditions and callbacks, she landed her first
role in Jean Anouilh's *Antigone*, a modern adaptation
of the ancient Greek tragedy written by Sophocles.
Angela played Antigone, a young woman who
refused to obey the unjust laws of her king and
instead chose to follow a higher moral code,
although it meant sacrificing her life.

The Negro Ensemble Company, seen here during a performance, had long been a source of pride for Angela and she was greatly influenced by the group's history.

Broadway director George C. Wolfe remembers seeing Angela's performance in that play. "To this day I can recall the sensation of sitting in that cold, dark theater, watching Angela work. I remember being rendered powerless by the endless swirl of contradictions that was her performance: absolutely in control, yet the essence of vulnerability; sensual, delicate, provocative . . . fierce! And what she was doing to that language—kissing and caressing it one minute and then spitting it out with haughty disdain the next."

After *Antigone* closed, Angela toured the United States with the Negro Ensemble Company (NEC), one of the oldest theater groups in New York dedicated to performing and promoting black theater. It was a happy coincidence that she found herself working with them. As a Yale undergraduate, Angela had written her thesis on the history of the Negro Ensemble Company.

This was a very exciting time in Angela's life. She joined the Actors' Equity Association, which gave her professional status and union benefits. Traveling and performing in Louisville, Cincinnati, and many cities in upstate New York, Angela served as the understudy in two NEC productions: *Colored People's Times* and Shakespeare's *Henry IV, Part I.*

Angela recalls on one occasion having to fill in and sing, "Do Nothing 'Til You Hear from Me." Acting she could handle, but the thought of singing in front of a large audience gave Angela her first case of stage fright.

When she wasn't traveling with the NEC, Angela found work on the soap opera *Guiding Light*. Around this time, Lloyd Richards, her former professor at the Yale School of Drama, called Angela with an important question. Would she be available to act in a couple of Broadway plays?

Richards was considered one of the most influential directors in American theater. In 1959, when he directed Lorraine Hansberry's *A Raisin in the Sun* on Broadway, he had made history by becoming the first black director of the first play written by an African-American woman to be produced on Broadway. Since that time, he had worked tirelessly to bring works by black playwrights to the stage. Angela knew that working for Richards on Broadway would establish her as an artist, if not a star.

For Richards' part, he had been so impressed with Angela's talent and beauty when she was a student at Yale that he kept her in mind when it came time to cast two August Wilson plays he was producing: *Ma Rainey's Black Bottom* and *Joe Turner's Come and Gone*. At that time, no one knew that the pairing of Richards and Wilson would be the beginning of one of the most important collaborations in American theater. Richards eventually produced five of August Wilson's critically acclaimed plays.

Ma Rainey's Black Bottom was voted best play of the year (1984–1985) by the New York Drama Critics' Circle. Three years later, in April 1988, *Joe Turner's Come and Gone* opened on Broadway to enormous critical acclaim, and it too received the Critics' Circle award for best play of the year. Angela played the character of Martha Pentecost in that play, a kind, loving, and long-suffering wife

The streets of Broadway are alive with the activity of people who regularly visit the many theaters found there. Angela had great success working on Broadway, but she still dreamed of being noticed by Hollywood.

whose hopes for happiness are destroyed by the unjust imprisonment of her husband. Although Angela had successfully established herself in New York theaters, she had Hollywood dreams, and was about to face the next transition in her life. Angela explains, "In New York, being successful means you've got an apartment that's not an illegal sublet. I wanted more. It's just part of my make-up to want something more."

Angela recalls the exact date—October 11, 1988—she left New York City for Hollywood, giving herself just six months to make it. "I guess I remember it because it was almost like starting over again," she told *Newsday*. "Like being a freshman. You're back at the bottom. They have to get to know you. Learn to trust you. You have to make that climb all over again."

What motivated Angela to make that move was a strong desire to be in movies or to land a role on a television series. "Then my family could rest assured; they wouldn't have to worry. If they see you on a weekly show, they can say: 'She's okay, you know they must be paying her.'" If it didn't work out, she told herself, she could always go to business school or teach.

Angela never had to use her contingency plans. Within a month of moving to California, she was cast in the Avery Brooks TV series *A Man Called Hawk*. She played the part of Hawk's girlfriend. Angela's mother was thrilled when the show aired.

After a brief run, the series ended and Angela found herself offered small roles on a variety of television series, including *227, The Cosby Show, Thirty-something, Tour of Duty,* and *Equal Justice.*

Angela soon received a call from film director John Sayles, who offered her a small part in *City of Hope*, a movie depicting the corruption and immorality of various characters in a city of very little hope. Angela played the conventional wife role.

Angela understood what such a role meant—the fact that working and playing a part, however small, got her name and face before the public. Slowly she was climbing that ladder to success. After *City of Hope* came a chance to audition for John Singleton's 1991 movie *Boyz N the Hood.*

John Singleton was still enrolled at the University of Southern California Film School when he signed on with the Creative Artists Agency. Upon graduating, Tri-Star gave Singleton a $6-million budget to make *Boyz N the Hood*, a film about three childhood friends growing up in the violent world of an inner-city ghetto. The main character, Tre, must choose between childhood ties that bind him to a life of senseless violence and the chance to break away and find something better. In the movie, Angela plays Tre's mother, a strong, determined woman who ultimately decides to hand her son over to his father (Laurence Fishburne) so he can teach him how to be a man.

John Singleton, the youngest director to ever be nominated for best director by the Academy Awards, gave Angela a chance to prove herself in his film and helped her open the door for her next role with director Spike Lee.

For John Singleton, *Boyz N the Hood* gave him the distinction of replacing Orson Welles as the youngest director to be nominated for an Oscar. For Angela, her powerful portrayal got her noticed in Hollywood and led to her next role. At that time, Singleton's mentor was Spike Lee, a young radical director who was about to begin auditions for *Malcolm X*, his most ambitious movie yet.

Considered one of the most important directors in modern American filmmaking, Lee exploded onto the movie scene in 1989 with his unsettling film *Do the Right Thing*. Since then he had directed several films.

Lee was determined to make a film based on the best-selling book *The Autobiography of Malcolm X* (1964), which was cowritten with Alex Haley. Angela had tried since her arrival in Hollywood three years earlier to get an audition with Spike Lee. When she eventually met Lee at a party, she approached him and with her characteristic determination announced that someday she'd like to work for him. Because of her recent success in *Boyz N the*

Hood and her connections with John Singleton, she got the chance to audition for the only prominent female role in *Malcolm X*—that of Betty Shabazz, Malcolm X's wife, who was also a nurse, teacher, and the mother of their six children. "I really wanted to play this role," Angela said. "I had read Malcolm X's autobiography when I was in college. It was the first thing I picked up in the morning, and the last thing I put down at night. To have the opportunity to play his wife—it's just amazing."

Denzel Washington played Malcolm X in the movie and was nominated for an Oscar for his outstanding portrayal of the charismatic leader. The role was particularly challenging because he had to play Malcolm as he changed over a 40-year time span. Washington hoped his portrayal would destroy the myth of Malcolm X being a violent man. "He wasn't violent," Washington explained in an interview. "Malcolm said if someone is blowing up your church and killing your babies and lynching your father, and your government is unwilling to protect you, then you should protect yourself. That's not violence. That's intelligence."

But there were constant troubles during production—with funding, with studio executives, and with Black Muslim leaders. By the end of filming, Lee had run over budget and the studio threatened to close production down. Lee appealed to several of his high-profile friends: Bill Cosby, Michael Jordan, Oprah Winfrey, Janet Jackson, Prince, Magic Johnson, and Tracy Chapman all contributed money to pay for two months of post-production costs until the movie was finished.

Critics described Angela's performance in *Malcolm X* as magnetic, assertive, and intelligent. Once again, she had taken a supporting role and turned it into something larger. Malcolm X's widow, Betty Shabazz, praised Angela's portrayal of herself as a strong, determined woman.

Dressed in white, Angela is seen here with Denzel Washington in a scene from Malcom X. In the film Angela played the role of Betty Shabazz, Malcolm X's wife.

Soon after finishing *Malcolm X*, Angela was thrilled to have the opportunity to play another real-life person—Katherine Jackson—mother of nine children, five of whom became the Jackson Five—in a television miniseries called *The Jacksons: An American Dream.*

As a young girl, Angela had been a fan of the Jackson Five. Not in her wildest dreams could she have imagined that someday she would be playing their mother. "That was the only group my mother paid money to have outfits made to go to their concerts," Angela told the *Los Angeles Times*, "When I was twelve my mother asked, 'What do you want for Christmas?' 'I want a guitar like Jermaine Jackson's.' I took lessons until the money ran out. I grew up with the Jackson Five."

The Jackson Five, according to Angela, were a positive influence on the black community because of their rags to riches story. From a life of poverty in the steel town of Gary, Indiana, to reaching the top of the Billboard charts in the record industry, the Jackson Five were a true American success story.

Playing Katherine Jackson was challenging for Angela for two reasons. Trying to portray a living person, capturing her mannerisms and personality, would be the most difficult type of acting. In addition, Angela would have to portray Katherine over a 40-year period, from the ages of 15 through 55. Fortunately, Angela was able to meet Katherine Jackson on the sets in Pittsburgh and Los Angeles. There, Angela received insight and suggestions from the Jackson matriarch herself. "She knows her own mind," Angela said. "She made some points to me."

The highly rated, five-hour miniseries would give Angela her first major television role. After playing the two highly acclaimed roles of Betty Shabazz and Katherine Jackson, Angela joked in an interview, "I think I have been incredibly blessed and it is probably just all downhill from here!"

Angela was mistaken. A fiery maven of rock and roll was looking for an actress to star in her life story. Would Angela have what it would take to answer the call?

4

WHAT'S LOVE GOT TO DO WITH IT?

T HE CALL WENT out throughout Hollywood. Tina Turner, goddess of rock and roll, would be bringing her harrowing yet ultimately triumphant life story to the big screen. The story spanned more than four decades—from Tina's days as an innocent country girl singing in the church choir in Nutbush, Tennessee, to her comeback tour in the concert halls of England and all the rhythm and blues dives in between. Playing Tina Turner would be a great acting challenge for any actress.

Tina's autobiography *I, Tina* was a best-seller in 1986. It told the story of Anna Mae Bulluck's transformation at the hands of Ike Turner into the star Tina Turner. Unfortunately, the more success Tina experienced, the more abusive, controlling, and violent Ike became. Eventually, Tina was forced to escape with nothing but her name and 32 cents in her pocket. She divorced Ike and successfully rebuilt her career, hitting it big with her 1982 Grammy Award–winning album *Private Dancer*. Ultimately, it would take seven years, three screenwriters, seventeen script rewrites, two directors, and a payoff of $45,000 dollars to Ike Turner (for signing a waiver not to sue over the film's portrayal of him), to get the movie into theaters.

But one of the greatest challenges in making the film would be finding the right actress to play Tina Turner. Every black actress in Hollywood wanted the part. Whoever won the role would need incredible

A scene from the 1993 film What's Love Got to Do with It?, *in which Angela transformed herself into a striking representation of Tina Turner.*

What's Love Got to Do with It? was based on an autobiography written by Tina Turner. Turner's life was turbulent, particularly when she was still involved with her ex-husband, Ike.

range and talent to play Tina from the age of 15 to 53. It was a rare opportunity, considering Hollywood didn't offer many roles for black leading ladies to begin with.

Halle Berry, Robin Givens, and Angela Bassett were the three finalists for the part. Auditions were grueling and lasted for over a month. Determined to give it her best shot, Angela worked with choreographer Michael Peters. Together, Peters and Angela studied hours and hours of videotapes from Tina Turner's performances. They would focus on one aspect of Tina's body and her mannerisms and try to nail it down. First the lips. How does Tina move them when she sings? Then Angela would practice Tina Turner lips until she had them perfect. Next, fingers and hands. What does Tina do with them when she's performing? Over and over again, Angela watched the tapes and learned how to move, dance, and sing like Tina Turner.

Angela recalls how difficult the auditions were: "They gave you six songs, including "Proud Mary" top to bottom. They gave you four or five scenes—young Tina, '60's Tina, '70's Tina, dragged down the hall and get a fractured left hand Tina. It was rough." And Angela really did fracture her hand during auditions. But her ability to give herself completely to the part, her uncanny resemblance to Tina Turner, and her hard work in mastering Tina's mannerisms and singing style paid off when she was awarded the role. Angela's previous success with playing real-life characters, Betty Shabazz and Katherine Jackson, helped to make her a logical choice as well. But playing the sexy Tina Turner would be entirely different from playing the nurturing mother roles of Shabazz and Jackson.

Angela told *Essence* magazine about the first time she met Tina on the set:

> When I walked into the room, she immediately hugged me and told her manager that she thought I was beautiful. And then she started showing me some of the dance routines from her days with the Ikettes (the background singers and dancers). Once you really get to know Tina, you see that she's just a warm, down-to-earth person. Her sex goddess image is only a public persona. In fact she's a dedicated performer who loves what she does for a living. Seeing her energy, her serious work ethic and just how beautiful she really is up close was all the inspiration I needed to be able to take on anything. When I walked out of that room, I was flying on cloud nine and I knew I would give the part everything I had!

Angela did just that—soaking her feet after 17-hour days of shooting the "Proud Mary" number in three-inch heels, practicing her lines and lip synching to Tina Turner's songs with precision, working with the choreographer to make sure the 12 dance numbers in the movie were as close to perfect as possible. And through it all, Tina Turner was there to offer advice and help.

Angela Bassett's portrayal of singer Tina Turner in What's Love Got to Do with It? *was so authentic that a film critic said it was as if Bassett were walking in Tina's shoes.*

Angela told *Ebony,* "When Tina came to the set she could have sat back, but she helped me with my make-up. She took the wigs, cut them for me, went to the store and bought shoes for me. She's so generous and loyal."

For one scene, Tina literally gave Angela the shirt off her back. Angela was rehearsing the number "I Might Have Been Queen" and she was wearing a little peach-colored T-shirt. Tina said, "Oh, that's so old-fashioned," and then she took off her white linen Armani shirt and said Angela should wear that instead. This attention to detail paid off. Critics praised *What's Love Got to Do with It?* as one of the best music biographies, ranking up there with the films made about Billie Holiday, Loretta Lynn, and Buddy Holly.

Laurence Fishburne, however, had a difficult time in his role as Ike Turner. Ike was definitely the villain in the movie. Yet, Fishburne somehow managed to take a character that wasn't fully developed and humanize him so the audience could see why he behaved as he did. Fishburne unexpectedly got the chance to meet Ike during filming. Although Ike was not welcome on the set, he nevertheless showed up one day in a limousine and handed out auto-graphed pictures. Ike showed Fishburne his walk and told him to do a good job playing him.

Fishburne did such a good job that he turned a role that was originally cast as a sup-porting part into a Best Actor nomination. Critics noted that the chemistry between Angela and Laurence was electric. Fishburne said of Angela, "She was the main reason I changed my mind about doing the movie. She's one of the greatest actresses to come along. I felt my job was to come in and really support her and let her know that every step she took, someone was there to catch her."

When playing scenes of abuse in the film, Angela knew she would be facing the most challenging scenes in her entire acting career. It really helped her to know that underneath Laurence's brutal character, he was in reality Angela's biggest supporter. "Brutality was a big part of Ike and Tina's relationship," Angela said in an interview after the movie was com-plete. "I trust Larry as a friend and actor. It's been a wonderful collaboration because I know he's not going to hurt me."

The superbly acted and choreographed musical performances in *What's Love Got to Do with It?* would become some of the best rock and roll scenes ever recorded in a movie. Fishburne did all of his own singing, but Angela lip-synched Tina Turner's songs in the movie—so convincingly that it's difficult to tell that Angela is not really singing.

Film critic Roger Ebert offered this assessment: "Bassett's performances of the songs are so much in synch—not just lip-synch, but physically, and with personality and soul—that it always seems as if we're watching Tina at work." For Ebert, the most harrow-ing scene of the movie comes the night Ike beats Tina

One of the main reasons that Angela and Laurence Fish-burne showed such chemistry on screen was due to the friend-ship they developed while work-ing on Boyz N the Hood, from which Fishburne, who played the father of the main character, is seen in this still.

The role of Tina Turner proved to be a breakthrough for Angela. Scripts started to roll in, and Hollywood began offering high salaries to Angela that showed how much they respected her as an actress.

yet once again, and the bleeding and battered woman walks out of their hotel, down a highway, and into a Ramada Inn. There she says, "My name is Tina Turner, and my husband and I have had an argument. I have thirty-two cents in my pocket. If you give me a room I promise you I will pay you back as soon as I can." The manager gives her a room. The Ramada Inn roadside sign is prominent in the scene in the movie because, as Tina wrote in her autobiography, she will forever be grateful to the motel for taking her in.

Ultimately *What's Love Got to Do with It?* is a movie of triumph and hope, as Tina breaks away from Ike and succeeds on her own. For Tina, helping Angela with her role in the film gave closure to this part of her life. However, when the movie was released she felt differently about actually sitting down and viewing it. When asked by *Time* if she planned on seeing the film, she said, "Do you think I want to see Ike Turner hit somebody again? It's not enough that I was hit. Now I have to watch him hit somebody else? I don't need to see this movie, 'cause I saw it already. I lived it."

Although Angela did not win an Oscar for the film, the nomination itself confirmed her talent. And numerous other awards for her performance in the film would follow: a Golden Globe Award for Best Performance by an Actress in a Motion Picture (Musical or Comedy) and an Image Award for Outstanding Lead Actress in a Motion Picture. Angela was also nominated for an MTV Movie Award for Best Female Performer, and the song "I Don't Wanna Fight" was nominated for a Grammy Award for Best Song Written Specifically for a Motion Picture or for Television.

After the release of *What's Love Got to Do with It?*, fans came up to Angela on the street. She had become a celebrity. For a woman who had been acting for more than 12 years, it was a strange feeling for people to suddenly approach her, reaching out and touching her arm as if they knew her.

Hollywood studios began sending Angela scripts, and she could command a salary into the six-figure range, the kind of payment that only a handful of black actors have ever commanded. Angela hoped with the success of *What's Love Got to Do with It?* that she would begin receiving opportunities to act in projects that didn't necessarily cast her according to race. But Hollywood has always been notoriously slow to change, and Angela faced the same struggles that many pioneering black actresses faced before her: the search for dignified, meaningful roles.

5

WHAT'S RACE GOT TO DO WITH IT?

❧

I F YOU ARE a black female and want to become an actress, what do you think your odds are of making it in Hollywood? What do you think your chances of having had a successful career in the 1940s or 1950s would have been? If you answered, "Slim to none," you would be correct. Yet a few early pioneering black actresses—Eartha Kitt, Lena Horne, and Dorothy Dandridge among them—managed to defy the odds. In a time when there were very few roles for women of color, these actresses found success in Hollywood films. Granted, they played showgirls, maids, and other stereotypical parts, but they paved the way for later stars like Ruby Dee, Rosalind Cash, and Cicely Tyson. During the 1970s, black actresses appeared in what were later called "blaxploitation" films: urban action dramas where the occasional female protagonist is able to overcome dire circumstances. Diana Ross's 1978 performance in *Lady Sings the Blues* marked a departure from the roles previously available to a black actress. Here, finally, was a strong, beautiful black woman, who was not a victim and who could hold her own with the likes of Billy Dee Williams.

Angela Bassett has faced many of the same struggles that black actresses faced in the past. A big part of the problem has been that Hollywood is a predominantly white-male owned and operated entertainment industry. Nowhere is this more evident than

African-American actors— female or male—still face employment hurdles in Hollywood. Of all the actors working in Hollywood, only a small percentage of movie roles are written for blacks. In this photo, actors Jeff Goldblum and Laura Dern pose with Angela.

47

when it comes to the Academy of Motion Picture Arts and Sciences, best known for its annual Oscar presentations. There have been only six black actors who have won an Oscar. The first was Hattie McDaniel, who won in 1939 for her role as the maid in *Gone with the Wind*. Sidney Poitier won in 1963 and has been the only black to win in the Best Actor category. Cuba Gooding Jr., Denzel Washington, Louis Gossett Jr., and Whoopi Goldberg have won for Best Supporting Actor and Actress roles.

The Academy of Motion Picture Arts and Sciences decides who receives nominations in the various categories and then the more than 6,000 Academy members vote to determine the winners. Who are the members of the Academy?

Membership is by invitation only, issued by an Academy member in good standing representing the same specialty. For example, an Academy member who is an actor may invite only actors for membership; directors may invite only directors. The prospective member must meet other membership requirements and be approved by two boards before being inducted. In 1996 when *Jet* asked the Academy for its demographic make-up, the editors were told the Academy does not release that information because the membership is private.

But even if minorities had greater representation in the Academy, they would still have to deal with the lack of significant roles for blacks in movies and on television. For black women, the problem is particularly severe.

Angela Bassett paid her dues by playing many small stereotypical roles when she first came to Hollywood. She played a prostitute in the miniseries *Doubletake*, a prison inmate in the TV movie *Locked Up: A Mother's Rage*, and a flight attendant in the film *Kindergarten Cop*. According to Angela, it's always a struggle to find roles that are dignified and intelligent. She remembers Sidney Poitier's advice: "If you want to do quality, sometimes you have to wait for it."

Apparently, black women have a longer wait than others. Dianne Houston, the first black woman nominated for an Oscar in directing for her short film *Tuesday Morning Ride*, offers this explanation: "Black women historically have been presented as either subhuman or superhuman. Now, we are starting to emerge as simply human, and that's a wonderful thing."

Unfortunately, for some of the most talented black actresses, one successful box-office hit doesn't necessarily open the door to better roles. Cicely Tyson did not get any major film roles after receiving an Oscar nomination for *Sounder*.

Veteran TV actress Ellen Holly told *Essence*, "Hollywood has perfected the formula of the white male hero with the white girlfriend and the black male mentor, or sidekick, with no visible love life. Where is the black woman in this?" A good example of this type of casting is found in the movie *The*

The cast of The Legend of Bagger Vance *pose for a photo (from left, Charlize Theron, Matt Damon, Will Smith) during the film's Hollywood premiere. Critics bashed the film for its stereotypical portrayal of the relationship between blacks and whites.*

Legend of Bagger Vance (2000). Christopher John Farley of *Time* calls it "One of the most embarrassing movies in recent history. Will Smith plays a magical black caddie who helps Matt Damon win a golf tournament and the heart of Charlize Theron. In 1930s Georgia, no less. You'd think Smith would have used his powers to, oh, I don't know, stop a lynching or two. It's a sad day when the PGA is showcasing minority role models that are more inspirational than Hollywood's."

Farley lists other recent films that use stereotypical formulas: *What Dreams May Come, Family Man, The Green Mile, Remember the Titans,* and *Men of Honor.* In none of these Hollywood movies is there a substantial role for a black actress and in most there is no role at all. So, while black actors must contend with playing supporting roles to the white male leads in these films, black actresses don't have the opportunity to play anything at all; they're not even in the picture.

There is simply a supply and demand problem for black actresses. The fact that hundreds of talented black actresses answered the casting calls for the roles of Betty Shabazz, Katherine Jackson, and Tina Turner vividly illustrated that there are just too few roles available for the talent pool out there, which leaves many actresses little opportunity to work and display their talents.

Another problem in Hollywood for a black actress is the age of the few black leading men. Denzel Washington, Wesley Snipes, and Laurence Fishburne are in their thirties and forties, but they are usually paired in movies with women who are much younger than they are, sometimes 20 years younger. Actresses who are in their thirties and forties are thus automatically out of the running.

Of course, there are always exceptions to these trends. A notable one is Whoopi Goldberg. She has found a variety of roles and is very successful in Hollywood. She's even hosted the Academy Awards show a few times. But for the most part the characters she plays in her movies are variations on herself—the zany, comic genius that she is. No one else could play those parts except Whoopi Goldberg. And although she has received recognition for her work in some dramatic roles, she is most successful and rewarded by the movie-going audiences when she plays Whoopi.

Margaret Avery—a talented actress who has done everything from Shakespeare to the 1960s television series *Sanford and Son*—is a more typical example of the struggling black actress. After working for many years in supporting roles, the role of a lifetime came for her when she was cast as Shug, the beautiful blues singer in the film *The Color Purple*, based on the novel by Alice Walker. She received a Best Supporting Actress nomination for her performance. "After *The Color Purple*, I really got a jolt. I didn't work for a year and a half," Avery said in an interview.

> The parts that followed were never pivotal in taking me to another level. They just kept me working. You just save and invest and prepare for when it ends. I went up for one role and the casting directors said, 'This role calls for someone to speak excellent English. Can Margaret do that? We need her to speak without a dialect.' They don't say that to Meryl Streep just because she does a Polish accent in a movie. If I speak in a southern dialect, they think that's me. I can't be acting.

Sheryl Lee Ralph, an actress who plays the stepmother in the hit television series *Moesha* recalls that when she first got into the business, there were years that even the Hollywood NAACP, which recognizes black actors and actresses ignored by the Academy, had to omit the category of best actress. "So few of us had worked in film. It was one of the saddest periods on record. There was nothing. And it was only yesterday." Ralph explained her situation in an interview: "During my career, I've been criticized for being too dark, too light, too pretty,

Sheryl Lee Ralph has faced many of the same problems as Angela while working in Hollywood. She has expressed frustration at the lack of quality roles offered to black actresses.

too short, too tall, all because there are so few roles out there for black women. The moment finally came when I realized that it was time to make the effort to find the right projects for myself. And not just any role for the sake of working either, but meaningful roles about characters that are non-stereotypical." Ralph explained she turned down a lot of roles that had her playing a "Black-mama-on-the-corner," and she added, "I'm sick and tired of being offered roles as the smart best friend, the giver of advice, a modern-day version of Aunt Jemima."

Before Angela Bassett's breakthrough playing Tina Turner, the actress had turned down many of the same stereotypical roles. Angela told *Harper's*

Bazaar, "My agent says I turn down money faster than anyone he knows," Angela knew the type of roles she desired and, like Sheryl Lee Ralph, she was tenacious in going after the parts.

Ruby Dee knows what it is to act in stereotypical roles. For a good part of her career, which has lasted more than six decades, the only acting jobs available were roles as maids. From there she gradually found fuller characters, both on Broadway and in the movies. Ruby Dee has performed Shakespeare (*The Taming of the Shrew* and *King Lear*) and she has appeared in more than 25 films. One of her most memorable film roles was as Rachel Robinson, the baseball player's wife, in *The Jackie Robinson Story*.

Dee and her husband, actor Ossie Davis, who have been married for more than 50 years, have worked tirelessly in the struggle to combat prejudice in Hollywood. "It's a very frustrating life and career unless you keep fighting for the things you love and believe in," Dee told *Essence*. "The sanity is to find ways to be a human being and an artist despite the racism. And if you're lucky, you'll be a success."

If you think the Hollywood film industry has been a tough place to make a living for a black actress, consider the history of African Americans on television. Jack White of *Time* recalls the joy of seeing blacks on TV in the 1950s:

Ruby Dee has been involved in Hollywood for well over 60 years and has found that determination and a love for acting has helped her continue to work in the film industry.

> Blacks were so rarely on television that the mere sight of one was enough to produce pandemonium in our Washington neighborhood. 'Colored on TV,' someone would shout from the front porch, and all normal activity ceased as everybody within earshot rushed to the nearest set for a moment of electronic racial solidarity. If somehow you missed the event, you felt seriously deprived. At a time when the civil rights

movement was just beginning, seeing blacks on the tube made us feel more like a part of America. We wanted them to be there even if it meant settling for a demeaning sitcom like Amos 'n' Andy. Anything was better than nothing."

Years later, in 1975, the leaders from the Los Angeles Urban League met with ABC television network to complain about the lack of roles for blacks on television. They were told that a 12-hour miniseries depicting the story of African Americans in this country would soon air. The series would be based on Alex Haley's *Roots*, the best-selling novel about his African ancestry.

ABC executives secretly feared that *Roots* would be a financial as well as a ratings disaster. But according to Greg Braxton of the *Los Angeles Times*, "By the end of its run on eight consecutive nights, *Roots* had accomplished much more than just soothing the concerns of blacks desperate to see themselves and their stories on TV. It made history, becoming the highest-rated television program ever. It was estimated that half the U.S. population watched the drama, with approximately 100 million people tuning in to the final installment."

Roots is considered the turning point for the depiction of blacks on television. No longer could studio executives use the excuse that the audience isn't there for shows based on black experiences. Yet for all of the hope *Roots* brought to blacks, many feel it never reached its full potential.

There have been great strides made in television—in the 1980s *The Cosby Show*, and in the 90s *Roc*, *Family Matters*, *A Different World*, *The Fresh Prince of Bel-Air*, and *Moesha* have received praise for positive portrayals of blacks. However, for the most part, blacks have been confined to sitcoms and are absent from leading roles in the prime-time drama series.

Debbie Allen, director and actress in the hit series *Fame*, told *Black Elegance*, "When I first started working, the challenge was that there were no parts. I'm talking none. Then the number of roles for black women increased during the eighties because of their growing presence on productions like *The Oprah Winfrey Show* and *The Cosby Show*." On *The Cosby Show*, Allen's sister Phylicia Rashad played Claire Huxtable and helped create a new image of black women on TV. Despite the success of *The Cosby Show*, none of the one-hour dramas on any of the networks featured an African American in a leading role.

During the 1990s, Eriq LaSalle in *ER*, Della Reese in *Touched by an Angel*, James McDaniel in *NYPD Blue*, and Malik Yoba of *New York Undercover* received praise for their talent and contributions to their prime-time dramas. But they are not the main stars of the show. Very few black actors actually carry a one-hour drama series.

Hollywood is showing some encouraging signs of moving beyond the barriers of race. Black actors, such as Eriq LaSalle (left) on ER, and actresses continue to make steady strides in the industry.

Some encouraging signs became evident on three networks in the fall of 2000: the ABC high-profile medical drama *Gideon's Crossing*, which stars Andre Braugher and features a multiethnic cast; and Fox's *Boston Public*, a dramatic series about a struggling inner-city high school with a diverse cast led by Chi McBride, who plays the commanding but compassionate black principal.

Scott Sassa, NBC's West Coast president in charge of programming, said, "I think we have done a great job of adding a number of people of color to our casts in a meaningful way. But when we looked at this problem we felt that you can have as many minority actors as you want, but you have to have the words on the page to make it work. So we felt that attacking it at the writer level was the most important way to make a real change over time rather than just a cosmetic change."

But for black writers the challenges are sometimes even greater than those faced by black actors and actresses. A writer needs to be perceived as a writer, not just a writer of ethnic stories and scripts. Although white writers work on both white and black shows, black writers are often perceived to be suited only for black shows. As a result, African Americans are shut out from the majority of projects in the business.

Zara Buggs Taylor, executive administrator of employment diversity for the Writers' Guild of America, said, "A 1997 survey found only three staff writers of color working on top ten TV shows, including *Suddenly Susan*, *NYPD Blue*, and a freelance Latina writer on *ER*. I hear about racism on the set all the time. Hollywood prides itself on liberal attitudes, but it's really an old boy's club in denial. People want to complain, but don't come forward because they're afraid they'll be fired or blackballed out of the industry."

According to Taylor, even more disturbing is the fact that "even though the majority of black TV writers work on black-themed shows, 70 to 75 percent of the writers on those shows are white males under the age of 40." Again, where does that leave the black female writer in all of this and might it explain why it's so difficult for actresses, black or white, to find decent roles?

LeVar Burton, who played Kunta Kinte in *Roots*, offered a solution to the *Los Angeles Times*: "The inclusion of blacks in the industry will not improve until we get into ownership."

Angela Bassett found a way to persevere despite the racism and sexism in Hollywood. In 1994, Terry McMillan was about to bring her best-selling novel *Waiting to Exhale* to the big screen. Once again, every black actress in Hollywood imagined herself playing one of the four leading female roles. After reading the book, Angela felt an immediate connection with one of the characters, the feisty Bernadine.

6

WAITING TO EXHALE

THE LONG LINES wrapped around lobbies and spilled onto the sidewalks at theaters across the country during the Christmas holiday weekend in December 1995. Groups of African-American women talked, laughed, and eagerly waited for the doors to open on the much anticipated film *Waiting to Exhale*.

Commentator Bebe Moore Campbell of National Public Radio said that "African-American women are going to see *Exhale* with such enthusiasm because they are starving for images of themselves on the big screen, in much the same way they were hungry to see their lives in books. And they're anxious to talk about what they see, just as they form book clubs to discuss what they read. The fact that so few films are done about women, and even fewer with African-American women, make even more acute the yearning to make *Exhale* an event."

In making the movie, McMillan was faced with the daunting challenge of transforming her novel into a screenplay. According to the *Los Angeles Times*, McMillan had become known for her "sister-circle signature style of storytelling: her perfect pitch and golden ear and reliance on heart and voice to propel a story." Writing a novel was something she knew how to do. Writing a screenplay would be an entirely different matter. At that time McMillan was busy promoting her book. She told *Essence*, "I had

Waiting to Exhale, *the film adaptation of black author Terry McMillan's novel by the same name, featured four black women in leading roles. Bassett's acting skills secured her a part in the 1995 film.*

Terry McMillan, the author of Waiting to Exhale, *worked diligently to maintain the essence of her characters in the film.*

been traveling for four months straight, promoting my book, and I didn't have time to spend with my son or open my mail. I was exhausted. The last thing I wanted to do was write a screenplay. I told them to get another writer."

Fox did, but when McMillan read the screenplay for *Waiting to Exhale*, she didn't like what the writer had done to her characters. A disappointed McMillan realized that she would have to cowrite the screenplay if she was to preserve her vision of the story for the movie. The writer she would collaborate with was Ron Bass, whose screenplays included the Academy Award–winning *Rain Man* and *The Joy Luck Club*. Eventually, after some altering of the story line, the screenplay for *Waiting to Exhale* was ready. McMillan now had to find a director and to begin the search for the four actresses who would play the parts of Savannah, Bernadine, Gloria, and Robin.

For directing duties, McMillan chose Forest Whitaker, a stocky, six-foot-tall former college-football player known for both directing and for his work in front of the camera. His acting credits included *The Crying Game*, *Jason's Lyric*, *A Rage in Harlem*, and *Bird*. "He's intuitive and sensitive, and he liked these women," McMillan said. "He didn't come into the project with some other agenda."

With Whitaker on board as director, the casting calls went out to fill the four staring roles. Black actresses knew this would be an opportunity of a lifetime. *Waiting to Exhale* was only the second major motion picture in recent years adopted from an African-American woman's novel. In 1985 it was Alice Walker's *The Color Purple* that had raised the hopes of many black actresses.

"I definitely saw Whitney Houston as the character Savannah," Whitaker told *Essence*. The recording star had already made her acting debut in the 1992 film *The Bodyguard*. With millions of fans eager to see Houston in another film, Twentieth Century Fox was thrilled to learn she wanted the part. Houston told *Essence*, "I loved the character in the book and I had always loved Forest Whitaker's work, so that initially attracted me to the project." Whitney would be playing the part of tall, sexy Savannah Jackson, a woman who returns to Phoenix from Denver to pursue a career as a television producer and reconnect with her friend Bernadine. Houston would also sing on the movie's soundtrack to cuts composed and written by Kenneth "Babyface" Edmonds. Toni Braxton, Aretha Franklin, Patti LaBelle, Chaka Khan, and Mary J. Blige were also invited to contribute their superstar power to *Exhale*'s soundtrack.

Terry McMillan had Angela Bassett in mind to play Bernadine—the wealthy, neglected housewife who finds out her husband is leaving her for his secretary. Whitney said, "I definitely wanted to work with Angela. I knew that with an actress of her caliber involved in the project, we would have a great movie. And, believe me, she plays the mess out of Bernadine!"

Angela had first met Terry McMillan three years earlier, at the premiere for *Malcolm X* in New York. The book *Waiting to Exhale* had just been published and there was already talk of making it into a movie. McMillan had asked Angela to play the part of Savannah. "No, I want to do Bernadine," Angela recalls telling McMillan. "I was attracted to her character."

Anyone who knows Angela will understand why. Out of the four characters in the book, Bernadine changes the most from the beginning to the end of the plot. She travels the more intense emotional journey and displays a wider range of feelings. By story's end, Bernadine turns her pain into triumph and ends up a stronger person.

Angela wore a pixie-cut wig and hazel contact lenses to play Bernadine. In the most riveting scene of the movie, Bernadine throws the contents of her husband's closet into his BMW, pours gasoline over it, and sets it on fire. Angela's range as an actress is clear, as it is in another emotionally charged scene where she has a conversation in a hotel bar with Wesley Snipes, a man whose wife is dying of cancer.

With Savannah and Bernadine set, Whitaker needed to cast the final two characters, Gloria and Robin. "The opportunities for Black actresses are much more limited than for other actors," explained Whitaker to *Essence*. "So, I wanted to give the roles to lesser-known actresses. I hope the success of this film will create more opportunities for Black actresses. They are the most under-used talents in the acting profession."

Whitaker cast Loretta Devine, a 20-year acting veteran best known for her role in the Broadway musical *Dreamgirls*, to play the part of Gloria, the single mother and hairdresser who finds love with her new neighbor, played by Gregory Hines. Devine says of the role, "I was very calm about the whole thing. I went through the drama of wanting a role so badly I could have died when *The Color Purple* came out. Never again." Whitney Houston remembers seeing the show *Dreamgirls* in New York when she was 15 years old, "Loretta was starring in *Dreamgirls* and I had seen the show several times and met her backstage. She was amazing."

The role of Robin Stokes, the sexy siren who falls for the wrong men, went to Lela Rochon, an actress who had appeared in the movie *Boomerang* and the television sitcom *The Wayans Brothers*. The competition for *Waiting to Exhale* was so intense that Rochon initially couldn't even get in to audition for the part. But she refused to give up and began a letter-writing campaign to Whitaker asking for an audition. Rochon told *Essence*, "I'd never done anything like that before, but I had read *Waiting to Exhale* when it came out and I just knew I was Robin." Whitaker agreed.

The director now had to finalize the supporting cast of men, which would include Dennis Haysbert, Mykelti Williamson, Leon, Kelly Preston, Bill Cobbs, Wendell Pierce, and Gregory Hines, as well as Wesley Snipes in a cameo appearance.

The entire cast of Waiting to Exhale *appear sitting together in front of a couch. They are, from the left, Loretta Devine, Whitney Houston, Bassett, and Lela Rochon.*

Whitney Houston, right, seen here in a scene from Waiting to Exhale *with Angela, was very nervous before the shoot and looked to the other more experienced actresses for advice.*

Shooting was scheduled for ten weeks in Phoenix, Arizona. From the very beginning the actresses and all involved with the project realized the historical importance of *Waiting to Exhale*. For the first time the lives of four black working women would be portrayed on the big screen. Angela said of this role, "This is the first time I've worked on a film where so many aspects of black women's lives are explored on-screen. We've all been in awe of the way the four of us have come together and truly become friends. That doesn't always happen on a set."

Houston, the least experienced actress of the four, was particularly nervous the night before shooting began. She was first on the shooting schedule in the morning. The cast and crew had gathered at a local bowling alley the night before to relax and get to know one another. Whitney told *Essence*, "I remember telling Angela, Loretta, and Lela how nervous I was. Angela said, 'Just go in there and do it.' My sisters were most encouraging and I won't ever forget that."

The movie encompasses a full year, from one New Year's Eve to another, and follows the lives of four friends as they cope with the trials and tribulations in love, marriage, parenting, and friendship. McMillan hoped that this film would bring about discussion on how sometimes women don't make the best choices in terms of choosing men who are right for them. She told *Time*, "The bottom line is that people will do stupid things when they want to feel loved."

Both Whitaker and McMillan have heard critics complain that *Waiting to Exhale* has too many negative male stereotypes. But McMillan counters the criticism with the explanation that the book, although not autobiographical, is based on her many unfulfilling romantic relationships over the years. Bits and pieces of her experience are in all four of the main characters.

Angela hopes audiences watching *Waiting to Exhale* will "get some insight into relationships as friends and insight into relationships as lovers. We all want someone to love us. Sometimes it works and sometimes it doesn't. Friendship, whether platonic or romantic, is the foundation. And we forget that sometimes in our rush to be intimate and close."

When *Waiting to Exhale* debuted the Christmas weekend of 1995, it made $14 million and was the number one box-office draw. Contributing to *Exhale*'s success was the Los Angeles–based First Weekend Club, founded by Sandra Evers-Manly. The club's purpose is to grab Hollywood's attention by supporting selected African-American films at the box office in their first weekend of release.

The club mobilized its more than 5,000 members, each of whom was responsible for recruiting 10 more people nationwide to see *Waiting to Exhale*. "The First Weekend Club encourages

The story portrayed in Waiting to Exhale *of four unique African-American women struck a chord with audiences, and the film closed after earning well over $67 million.*

African-American film fans to support films that show blacks in healthy relationships and romances, films that show the importance of family," Evers-Manly told the *Los Angeles Times*. "If we want to make a difference, we've got to go out the first weekend. Money talks in Hollywood, and such financial advocacy is particularly effective."

Once a film has been screened and targeted, the club rallies to its support by making phone calls, sending faxes, and distributing flyers—in short, doing everything it can to ensure the film has a strong opening weekend. Some of the films it supported in the past are *Jackie Brown, Amistad, Rosewood, Hope Floats,* and *Deep Impact.* Support for a film is based not only on whether there are diverse black characters in a movie but also if African Americans direct the films.

Waiting to Exhale earned over $67 million, repeating the success of the novel, which stayed at the top of the best-seller list for nine months. Such figures demonstrated that a movie did not need to be targeted for whites to be a hit. The black audiences' support alone could make it one. Most importantly, *Exhale*'s success sent a clear message to Hollywood: black women's stories matter and are marketable, too.

Angela spoke with the *Toronto Sun* about her experience working on *Waiting to Exhale*. "If you have just one of those fabulous moments in your career, then that is pretty amazing. You always aspire to that level but you're not always going to make it. That was my Mt. Everest. I might not climb Mt. Everest two, three, four or ten times in my lifetime. But I can aspire to that and try to do good work."

7

HITS AND MISSES

❧

Following the success of Waiting to Exhale Angela was offered a wide range of roles. Some were quite successful while others didn't fare so well, but one area in which Angela found the greatest success was in her relationship with Courtney B. Vance.

ANYONE LOOKING FOR Angela Bassett in 1995 didn't have to look far. With the release of *Waiting to Exhale* and three other movies that same year, she could be seen in theaters across the country. Angela starred or had supporting roles in *Vampire in Brooklyn, Panther,* and *Strange Days.* She followed these three films with a supporting role in the hit *Contact,* released in 1997.

Charlie Murphy wrote *Vampire in Brooklyn* with his brother, actor Eddie Murphy, in mind. Murphy had experienced incredible success in the 1980s with the films *Beverly Hills Cop, Trading Places, 48 Hours,* and *Coming to America.* He was hoping that *Vampire in Brooklyn* would give him a new image and revive his career, which by the mid 1990s was flagging. Unfortunately, the movie encountered problems and tragedy from its very beginning.

When Paramount Pictures purchased the rights to the screenplay, they felt the script still needed a little work, so they called in script doctors—writers who specialize in fixing problem scripts. By the time the final version of *Vampire* was complete, it suffered from having too many writers involved, each with his own ideas about how the story should work. With all these different interpretations, *Vampire in Brooklyn* became far-fetched and disjointed. Even Wes Craven, the director of *Scream* and the *Nightmare on Elm Street*

One of Angela's films that didn't do very well in theaters was Vampire in Brooklyn. Angela shared the screen with Eddie Murphy in this horror/comedy, but the film did not appeal to a large audience.

films, couldn't bring coherency to what was now a comedy-horror movie.

Three days into filming, Angela's stunt double, Sonja Davis, died in a tragic accident. A shocked and saddened Angela told *Entertainment Weekly,* "I was there watching her. It was a scene where my character was supposed to jump from one building to another and not make it and fall through the roof of a car. . . . We were devastated."

LaFaye Baker, a Hollywood stuntwoman who had worked as a double for Angela in *What's Love Got to Do with It?*, came in as Davis's replacement. Baker knew the job of a stunt double could be dangerous, even fatal, but she had learned what a stuntwoman needed to know. "I had to learn fight scenes," she explained to *Essence,* "things like camera angles on throwing punches, because there actually isn't any contact. I learned how to do high falls and car-chase scenes and to work on an air ramp, an apparatus that propels you into the air with a ratchet that has a wire attached to it. We used that in *Vampire in Brooklyn* where I was doubling for Angela and came crashing through the floor. It helps that I have a background in gymnastics."

In the movie, Angela plays Rita, a beautiful New York Police Department detective, whose character is pursued by Maxmillian, a Caribbean vampire played by Eddie Murphy. Maxmillian comes to Brooklyn to find Rita, who he believes is destined to be his bride. All Maxmillian has to do is dance with Rita and bite her on the neck, which will thus bind the two of them together for eternity. But Rita has her own ideas. She's interested in her handsome partner, Justice, played by Alan Payne. When the two of them are assigned to investigate murders committed by Maxmillian, their romance develops.

Will Rita resist her destiny in becoming a vampire and Maxmillian's wife? Or will Rita and Justice find true love? Apparently, the movie audience didn't care enough to know, and *Vampire in Brooklyn* tanked at the box office, earning much less than what it cost to make the film. Angela said of the experience to the *Los Angeles Times*, "I had fun doing it, but wish it were done better!"

Angela's next role was a cameo appearance in the Mario Van Peebles film *Panther*. This was a dramatized account of the story of the Black Panthers, a militant organization of black youths in the 1960s, that had grown impatient with Dr. Martin Luther King's stance on passive resistance. They believed in protecting their own and encouraging blacks to have pride in themselves. In the film Angela briefly recreated the character of Betty Shabazz, the wife of Malcolm X, a role she had received critical acclaim for just three years earlier in Spike Lee's film *Malcolm X*.

Further proving her versatility as an actress, Angela tackled her first science fiction–action film, *Strange Days*, which also starred Ralph Fiennes, Tom Sizemore, and Juliette Lewis. In this futuristic tale of destruction, Los Angeles is set to be the center of the apocalypse. Fiennes's character, Lenny, is a cop turned bad guy. He deals in virtual reality chips, called squids, that offer people any experience without accountability or risk. Lenny is framed for a murder he didn't commit. Angela's character, Lornette "Mace" Mason, a tough karate-kicking bodyguard and Lenny's loyal friend, tries to help him find out who the real murderers are and bring them to justice.

Karen Bigelow, the director of *Strange Days*, told *Harper's Bazaar*, "Casting Bassett wasn't exactly a difficult decision. She's one of the most talented actresses

In the movie Strange Days, *in which Angela appeared with Ralph Fiennes, Angela proved that she could carry a wide range of roles including that of an action hero.*

working in the business today. If you want Angela to dial a performance down you just say so and she's right in the zone. And when a shot called for a Schwarzenegger moment, you just ask her to increase the volume and she'd go as far as you'd ever want to go."

Many critics thought Angela's role as Mace was the highlight of the movie. Jack Kroll of *Newsweek* said, "Bassett is Bigelow's trademark figure of female power rising above male inanity. Stunning, rippling-muscled Bassett turns a pulp persona into a heroic archetype."

Although *Strange Days* wasn't a box-office success, it provided further proof of the range of Angela's acting ability. From nurturing mother figures to science fiction–action heroine, Angela has played a variety of characters who are courageous, competent, and clever—qualities associated with Angela's own character and work ethic in Hollywood.

Angela's next movie, *Contact*, was another science fiction film, only this one was a big hit. Costarring with fellow Yale graduate Jodie Foster, Angela plays Rachel Constantine, a high-level advisor to the president and the official bridge between the White House and the scientists who discover a message from outer space.

Angela's character Rachel accepts the possibility that life exists on other planets—although Angela Bassett herself does not. Angela told the *Calgary Sun* in an interview, "I don't think there are aliens in our galaxy and I certainly have no desire to go on an expedition to find out one way or another. I love looking at the stars. I just don't want to visit them."

Based on Carl Sagan's best-selling 1985 novel, *Contact* tells the story of Dr. Ellie Arroway, an astronomer who intercepts a signal from aliens on the huge dish-shaped radio telescope near Socorro, New Mexico. The source of the signal turns out to be Vega, a star 26 light-years away. The countries of the world unite in an effort to decode the transmission. The message turns out to be detailed instructions on how to build a machine that will bring about the first contact between extraterrestrials and humans. Ellie vies to be selected as the single representative from earth to use the machine and the first person to make contact. Angela's character is one of the more important supporting roles in the film because it is Rachel's job to interpret the alien message Ellie brings back from space. She must keep its negative impact under control and protect the president from any political repercussions.

In an interview with *Jet*, Angela describes her character: "There's a part of Rachel that is a cheerleader for Ellie. But, as a woman who's had to earn the position she holds, Rachel also isn't going to let Ellie slide. If anything, she's going to make it a little bit more difficult, so that when Ellie rises to the challenge, everyone will know just exactly how much she's worth."

Angela and Jodie thoroughly enjoyed working together on this film. Bassett told the *Atlanta Journal*, "I was excited about being able to watch her [Foster] on

In the film Contact Angela played the role of one of the president's top aides as the world learns that there may be other intelligent life-forms in the universe.

the set daily because she's incredible. When you talk to lay women and men in the African-American community, they call her one of their favorite actresses."

Contact was produced by Robert Zemeckis and Steve Starkey, Oscar winners for Forrest Gump. They reunited virtually all of their award-winning team from that film, including director of photography Don Burgess, costume designer Joanna Johnston, and composer Alan Silvestri. Sony Imageworks created the fantastic visual effects for the film under five-time Academy Award–winner Ken Ralston. Principal photography on Contact began with a week of location filming at the VLA (Very Large Array), a field of 27 dish-shaped radio telescopes located in the desert of Socorro, New Mexico. The VLA is a facility used by astronomers to study the sun, planets, comets, stars, galaxies, and gas clouds throughout the universe. In the film much of Ellie's early research takes place at the VLA.

The filmmakers found it necessary to shoot the VLA in the fall to take advantage of the formation of the dishes when they were closest to one another. New Mexico filming was completed just as the dishes were scheduled to be moved into a new formation to follow the movement of the stars. Scenes from *Contact* were also filmed in Los Angeles; Washington, D.C.; Cape Canaveral, Florida; and Arecibo, Puerto Rico—the location of the world's largest radio telescope.

Roger Ebert of the *Chicago Sun-Times* said "*Contact* tells the smartest and most absorbing story about extraterrestrial intelligence since *Close Encounters of the Third Kind*." Angela feels the story is even more personal than that, "Although, it's a big story, It's really about people: why they do what they do, why they love each other and their relationship to the universe."

After finishing *Contact*, Angela decided to make a major personal commitment in her own life: to marry longtime friend and fellow actor Courtney B. Vance. Angela and Courtney had met 14 years earlier when they were students at the Yale School of Drama. They had been good friends ever since, enjoying each other's company whenever they were in town together.

When Angela was ill with the flu, Courtney was there for her, not only as a friend but also as a nurse and companion. "He made sure I had food and medicine and just took care of me. And he didn't ask anything. I'm usually the one who's doing the caregiving." Angela began to have feelings stronger than friendship for Courtney, but he was busy with his own career and thought Angela still wanted to continue as friends.

Courtney B. Vance has appeared in more than 20 movies—*Space Cowboys*, *Dangerous Minds*, and *The Hunt for Red October*, to name a few. But it was his role as the hardworking minister who neglects his wife and son in *The Preacher's Wife* that really had an impact on Vance. "This role came to me at this particular time in my life for a reason," he explained.

The reason, according to Vance, was that he needed to reconnect with religion in order to help

Having been longtime friends, Angela and Courtney B. Vance soon found that they were interested in one another romantically. Angela said of Courtney that in him she found all the qualities she was looking for in a husband.

him through a family tragedy. In 1990, Courtney's father committed suicide. Prayer and faith in a higher power helped pull Vance through this very painful time. Vance was working on the film *The Preacher's Wife* with Whitney Houston and Denzel Washington, when he decided to become baptized at the Abyssinian Baptist Church in Harlem—the same church he had attended in order to observe services in preparing for his role in the film.

Courtney, like Angela, first started acting in high school plays. He enjoyed acting but never thought it would become his career. Also like Angela, he worked hard in school and achieved excellent grades. After graduating from Harvard University and then taking a year off, he was accepted at the Yale School of Drama, where he met and became friends with Angela.

In an interview with the *Calgary Sun*, Angela described how she watched Courtney closely when she first met him. "He was such a gentlemen with everyone. He was a man who gave of himself so quickly and easily. He did such kind things for people like walking my best friend's mother's dog. The more I watched Courtney around other people, the more I knew he was the kind of man I could get through rough patches with and that was really important for me."

Angela knew Courtney had all the qualities she hoped to find in a husband. He was religious, generous, and intelligent. They had been friends for more than 14 years. The question was how she could convey to a longtime friend that she had fallen in love and wanted something more from the relationship? Angela said in an interview, "I had to give him an inkling that I was interested in more than friendship. Fortunately he picked up on my intentions pretty quickly."

Soon after, Courtney B. Vance got down on one knee and slipped a diamond ring on Angela's finger. The ring was the same one made in 1910 for his grandmother's engagement. On a clear autumn day, October 12, 1997, Angela Bassett and Courtney B. Vance were married in a quiet ceremony held at a private residence in Los Angeles. Two hundred and twenty-five family members and friends, including James Earl Jones and Lloyd Richards, attended the wedding. Angela wore a fitted silk Escada gown with a four-foot French lace train. Her three bridesmaids wore pale green organza gowns and matching coats with hand-embroidered sleeves, also designed by Escada.

The easy part was getting married. The challenge would be working through the hard times that all married couples face. The hard times for Angela and Courtney have been when they're apart from each other working on separate movie locations. They keep in touch and feel connected by talking on the phone every night. Angela told Joey Berlin of *Hollywood News*, "Two-celebrity relationships aren't easy. You have a light on you, you have more attention. You've got many, many more neighbors who are wondering how you're doing. But all relationships take effort. They'll all be tested. So just get ready, look for it and weather it."

Angela's next project would prove once again that she was up for challenges, whether in her personal life or career.

8
IN A GROOVE

*H*OW STELLA GOT *Her Groove Back* opened August 14, 1998, in 1,393 theaters across the country. It grossed an estimated $11.8 million in its first three days—only $1 million less than the leader that weekend, *Saving Private Ryan*, which opened in 3,000 theaters. *Stella*'s per screen tally of $8,500 per theater was significantly higher than that of any other films released that summer.

How Stella Got Her Groove Back is based on Terry McMillan's true-life romance with Jonathan Plummer, a Jamaican man more than 20 years her junior. In writing the screenplay for *Stella*, McMillan teamed again with Ron Bass, who helped write the screenplay for *Waiting to Exhale*.

Angela had known for four years that the part of Stella would be hers. While on the set for the filming of *Exhale*, McMillan was in the process of completing the book, *How Stella Got Her Groove Back*. She told Angela about the character and asked her to play the lead. Since that time, the script had gone through three rewrites, and a minor character in the book, Delilah, played by Whoopi Goldberg in the film version, would become Stella's sidekick and best friend.

McMillan's novel sold over two million copies based on the appeal of the older woman–younger man romance. In Hollywood films, it's not uncommon

Angela dances with Taye Diggs in a scene from the 1998 How Stella Got Her Groove Back.

Whoopi Goldberg, seen here with Angela in How Stella Got Her Groove Back, *added a comic touch to the film. Angela immediately felt very comfortable working with the famous comedian on the film.*

for a younger woman to be paired with a much older man. *Indecent Proposal, Disclosure, Runaway Bride,* and many real life Hollywood marriages are but a few examples. But *Stella* reversed that formula with the 40-year-old female lead, Stella, meeting the 20-year-old Winston while vacationing in Jamaica. They fall in love and that's when the problems begin.

Stella is a single mother and a successful stockbroker who has recently lost her job. Delilah encourages Stella to travel to the tropical sunshine for some relaxation and fun. Winston, played by Taye Diggs, is working as a part-time chef while he contemplates attending medical school, when he meets Stella at a Jamaican resort.

Once Stella and Winston decide to continue their romance beyond the vacation, the negative reactions from family on both sides force them to face the reality of their age difference. Winston's mother is only a year older than Stella and doesn't approve of the match. Stella's snippy sisters give her a difficult time as well. Even Stella begins to have doubts about falling in love with a younger man.

In McMillan's book, best friend Delilah is dead and exists only as a ghost Stella talks to. This created a problem in writing the movie version. How could Stella's thoughts and conflicts be brought out into the open and conveyed to the audience? That's where Whoopi's character, Delilah, comes in, providing a great deal of humor in the movie because she is the one who speaks the lines from the book that Stella only thinks in her head. She also serves as a foil to Stella's serious nature.

Angela told the *Washington Post*, "I'm so much the drama queen. So I don't think that I am funny on screen. It is such a difficult thing to be genuinely funny on screen, which is why I appreciated so much the scenes with Whoopi. But I didn't spend too much time sitting around thinking, 'How can I make this funny?' My thought is always, 'How can I make this honest?'"

Angela was thrilled when she learned that Whoopi Goldberg had agreed to play Delilah. "The first time I met her in a little restaurant a couple of months after I had moved to LA, I go over and say, 'Hi,' and she was so warm and so open," Angela told the *Los Angeles Times*. "I remember she looked me directly in my eyes, and she introduced me to the people that she was with. And she just engaged me in warm, genuine, sincere conversation."

With Whoopi playing Delilah, Angela felt the movie would have a good chance at being a hit. "She would just give so much of herself, so I was always so impressed," Angela said of Whoopi. "She made the relationship between Stella and Delilah so rich, and I don't think anybody else could have done it. And I don't know if it would have been as fun. Because of the type of person she is, she makes you feel so welcome and any intimidation just goes right out the window. You're up there, and you're rolling.

All of a sudden you think you're ready to be a standup comic!"

Taye Diggs was a newcomer to Hollywood when he won the part of Winston, Stella's boyfriend in the movie. Diggs was 27 at the time but looked younger. He had just finished playing Benny from the Broadway Pulitzer Prize–winning play *Rent*. Diggs had no previous film experience, and he initially found the differences between acting on stage and acting in a movie very challenging. "In theater, you get up there for two and a half-hours and you go straight through," Diggs explained. "In film, you could do a scene and then come back four weeks later and do, you know, the next day. So emotionally you have to get yourself back to that place."

Diggs honed his acting skills at a high school for the performing arts in Rochester, New York, and gained admittance to Syracuse University. There, he earned a Bachelor of Fine Arts in Musical Theatre and was promptly signed to an agency after an impressive performance as the understudy in the play, *Carousel*.

Angela was impressed with Diggs's performance as well as his personality. "He's just a very sweet person. When he talks with anyone on the set, he's just very easy with himself. If he doesn't know, he asks. He laughs easy, and he shares. I feel comfortable with people who are open and not standoffish. I was very excited for him that he was going to be a lead in this motion picture and it was a first for him. He looks great, he does a great job, and he's going to get a lot of attention."

Angela did not want attention from doing nude love scenes in the movie. So she refused to do them.

The clothes Angela refused to remove in the film were gorgeous Ruth E. Carter designs. Carter, a costume designer for the movies *Amistad*, *What's Love Got to Do with It?*, *Malcolm X*, *Do the Right Thing*, and *School Daze*, wanted Angela to have a different look for this film. Carter told the *Los Angeles Times* "that Angela always plays these wonderful role models, but they're very tough and structured and suited and tailored. I thought it was time to reverse that. I wanted to do glamorous the whole time."

Kevin Rodney Sullivan, who directed *Stella*, said Angela "has a real movie star presence. The cameras and costume designers love her. She looks spectacular in any outfit and in any light. It makes life easy for a director."

Sullivan had high praise for Angela's acting abilities as well. "Angela Bassett was perfect because of her range and depth. She has a life force, a soul, a spirit that is very powerful," Sullivan told *Black Elegance*. "Stella represents a three-dimensional character—sexy, funny, powerful. In the past black female characters have been limited—typically one thing or the other—never all. If audiences could see more African-American females in multidimensional roles, it would be wonderful."

McMillan feels it would be wonderful, too. Tired of hearing speculation about whether the movie would appeal to blacks as well as whites, she just wanted the work to speak for itself. But considering the types of stories featuring blacks in movies released before *Waiting to Exhale* and *How Stella Got Her Groove Back*, it's progress that a romance centering on black women made it to the big screen at all. The lack of success that critically acclaimed black films, such as *Eve's Bayou*, have received seems to prove McMillan's point.

"I wish more people would have gone to see *Eve's Bayou*," McMillan told the *Los Angeles Times*. "It's a beautiful film and we don't have very many films by African-Americans that are cinematically, and aesthetically, and philosophically, as moving and as powerful as that story. But because we're black and nobody is getting shot and chased and there's no drugs and not a lot of cussing, then all of a sudden we have critics saying, 'It's a little slow.'"

Some critics found *How Stella Got Her Groove Back* a little slow, if not unbelievable. Colin Covert

Taye Diggs, a relative new-comer to Hollywood when work began on How Stella Got Her Groove Back, *impressed Angela with his talents as an actor and with his charming personality.*

of the *Minneapolis Star Tribune* wrote, "The new science-fiction film, *How Stella Got Her Groove Back*, explores the romantic trials of a woman who lives in a galaxy far removed from our own. It's set on a planet where Angela Bassett can't find a date. As we know, on planet Earth, men would throw themselves at her feet until they formed a pile that would have to be removed by a backhoe."

Yet, even though the film had a weak plot, critics agreed that Angela's performance was the highlight of the movie. Steve Murray in the *Atlantic Journal* wrote, "Luckily, there's Bassett grounding the picture with a glowing performance, sharing with us Stella's unexpected moments of emotional rediscovery. She makes you believe things are happening, even when a scene is dead in the water."

How Stella Got Her Groove Back performed well at the box office and in the home video market, turning in respectable earnings. Released on video in early 1999, it has earned roughly $39 million in revenue.

How Stella Got Her Groove Back won the NAACP Thirtieth Annual Image Award for Outstanding Motion Picture. Angela won the Image Award for Best Actress and Whoopi Goldberg won for Best Supporting Actress. The island of Jamaica benefited as well. Since *Stella's* release, tourism, especially among American women, has increased by 22 percent.

In between movie projects, Angela had the opportunity in 1998 to return to her first love—theater. She played Lady Macbeth to Alec Baldwin's Macbeth at the Joseph Papp Public Theater in New York City. Angela said of the experience, "I hadn't been back to the stage in so long. I missed that intimate contact with a live audience, the way you get into the emotion of a character. In movies you're doing small moments again and again and again, building a scene. But there's something about the passion you bring to the stage, the way you have to be bigger on the stage and reach all the way to the back of the theater, and I could pull it back and shape it and do whatever I want with it."

With the exceptional talents of Angela and the other cast members, How Stella Got Her Groove Back *performed well in theaters and received recognition from the NAACP.*

Angela had come home to what had attracted her to acting in the first place. On stage is where it all began for her. "That's where I started. That's the way I grew up," Angela told the *Los Angeles Times*. "I remember when I used to audition for theatrical roles, and I would do anything! Jump on a fireplace, roll around, and shout. Whatever was needed. And that's such a wonderful difference from working in front of a camera, which is like working with a laser, as opposed to a scalpel, to get at a character."

As a teenager, Angela felt that all she wanted to do was make people feel the way James Earl Jones had made her feel sitting in the audience so many years ago. Judging from the critics' reviews, Angela has achieved her childhood goal. Sheryl Altman said of Angela's performance, "On stage, she was fire and fury, her teeth gnashing and Linda Hamilton-like biceps bulging. Critics likened her to a caged tiger preparing to pounce."

Linda Winer of *Newsday* wrote, "The headlines belong to Bassett. Returning to the stage after having her triumphant way with Hollywood and Tina Turner, the actress takes her first Shakespearean role in her teeth and wrestles it to the ground. Leonine, fearsome, glamorous, yet earthy, Bassett's Lady Macbeth seems quite capable of taking the throne away from all competitors without having to raise a dagger."

Linda Armstrong of the *New Amsterdam News* said, "Bassett is masterful in her performance of Lady Macbeth. While her evil is remarkably cruel at first and her ambitions for her husband overpowering, she truly loves him. Bassett has the audience completely mesmerized as she goes mad—sleep walking while talking of murder and continually and forcefully motioning to wash her hands, which could never be clean of the blood of those she forced Macbeth to slaughter. One had to feel pity for this evil character, who reaped the fate of her deeds."

In a unique performance of Macbeth, Angela and co-star Alec Baldwin threw conventional opinion aside about how blacks and whites should relate on stage.

The color-blind casting of Angela and Alec Baldwin was an unique aspect to this performance of *Macbeth*. George C. Wolfe—the director of the play, best known for his Tony Award–winning musical, *Bring in 'Da Noise, Bring in 'Da Funk*—cast a few other blacks in the play in addition to Angela. He told *Newsday*, "The opportunity to play all types of roles was hard won. Critics, producers, and writers are sometimes so rigid and literal in approaching what is about imagination, and heightened reality. They couldn't see beyond 'How can she be playing his sister if she's black and he's white?' Only when they saw that people weren't running screaming out of the theater did they come around. It's a wearing down process until you get to the point where you simply get the best possible actor for the role. We still have a long way to go, but we're getting there."

Angela's performance signaled her accomplishment. No longer was she offered roles based on being a black actress. She had crossed the color barrier and was now offered parts based on her extraordinary acting skills and the demand for strong female characters similar to what she had portrayed in the past.

In her next film, *Music of the Heart*, Angela would be working with a fellow graduate of the Yale School of Drama—Meryl Streep. "I have never been more nervous to meet anyone in my life," Angela said in an interview. About their characters' tense relationship in the movie, she added, "It was Meryl Streep, after all, and I was going to have to have a shouting match with her."

Angela didn't need to worry. She found Meryl to be down-to-earth, warm, and funny. It turned out that Meryl was a big fan of Angela's work. Streep told *Jet*, "I've idolized Angela for a long time, so I was really, really thrilled to work with her and to get to scream at her and have her scream back at me. We have a great relationship in this film."

Music of the Heart is the inspirational true story of a music teacher's struggle to teach violin to inner-city schoolchildren. Meryl Streep plays Roberta Guaspari, a recently divorced mother of two young sons who needs to find a job to support her family. Roberta approaches Janet Williams, played by Angela, the no-nonsense principal of an East Harlem elementary school, and asks for a job teaching violin to the students. The students are mostly underprivileged black and Hispanic children who are not expected to have the attention span to learn a difficult instrument like the violin.

Roberta is persistent and Williams is eventually won over and offers her a job. Angela said of her character, "Education is so important to her. Children really are our future and Janet, my character, sees that. She knows if you motivate them, if you love them, if you invest in them, if you discipline them, give them their boundaries and exposure to the world, then there's no limit to the great things they can do."

Once again, Angela found herself playing the tough female role with a soft heart. Williams eventually becomes Roberta's number-one supporter and helps her fight for the funding when the Board of Education cuts the music program. Angela said of the film, "In our day and age, we find that whenever the money gets short, the first things to get cut are the things that children tend to enjoy a great deal. . . . Not everyone can be a mathematician or a scientist or excel in English. But they may be an incredible artist or musician. I would say that *Music of the Heart* is about nurturing the creative spirit in our children."

In *Music of the Heart*, Angela worked once again with Wes Craven, who directed her in *Vampire in Brooklyn*. Also starring in the movie are Aidan Quinn, Cloris Leachman, and singer Gloria Estefan, making her feature film debut. The film also includes cameos by violinists Isaac Stern, Itzhak Perlman, and Arnold Steinhardt of the Guarneri Quartet. Bluegrass genius Mark O'Connor also makes an appearance at the end of the movie in the breathtaking Carnegie Hall concert scene.

Critics praised the movie. Ellen A. Kim of Hollywood.com wrote "The final concert scene is especially effective, not only for the delight of seeing violin legends stand alongside the children, but for the emotional forte of the setting. Most serious musicians have at least once dreamed of playing at Carnegie Hall, standing on the vast stage, buoyed only by applause. For Streep and her students, the dream becomes reality, and the applause is well deserved."

9

TIMING, TALENT, AND TENACITY

❦

IN 1999, ANGELA BASSETT was thrilled to once again have the chance to play a real-life heroine. She would be starring in *Wings Against the Wind*, the story of Bessie Coleman, dubbed "Queen Bess" by the press, the first black woman to fly an airplane and the first African American to earn an international pilot's license. In the 1920s women pilots were rare, a black woman pilot was unheard of. Doris Rich, in her book *Queen Bess: Daredevil Aviator*, wrote, "From the moment Bessie decided to become a pilot nothing deterred her. The respect and attention she longed for and her need to 'amount to something,' were directed at last toward a definite goal."

Coleman learned to fly in France where race was less of a barrier than in the United States. After seven months of instruction and a rigorous qualifying exam, Bessie Coleman received her license from Federation Aeronautique Internationale.

Coleman knew that in order to earn a living as an aviator she would have to become a stunt pilot and participate in air exhibitions across the country. Coleman's ultimate dream, though, was to open a flying school for African Americans. She worked tirelessly, giving speeches and performing exhibitions in order to raise the money to open the school. Tragically, during a routine practice flight, Coleman was thrown from her plane and she plunged to her death.

Angela Bassett has long understood that her dream of being an actress required a lot of hard work and heart. A long, successful career is proof that Angela's dream has come true.

Bessie Coleman, seen here in her plane, strived to give African Americans the opportunity to better themselves, but her dream was tragically cut short when she fell to her death in a flying accident. Angela felt honored to portray such a courageous woman on screen.

Thousands of people mourned her death, many of them women and children who had listened to her speeches. Black aviators inspired by her achievements formed a network of Bessie Coleman Aero Clubs. In 1992, the U.S. Postal Service issued a stamp commemorating her extraordinary life and accomplishments.

Angela Bassett worked with Danny Glover, Aidan Quinn, and Gerard Depardieu in *Wings Against the Wind*. Although the film wasn't a box-office hit, Angela took pride in bringing Coleman's story to the big screen.

Angela said in an interview, "I remember going to the Museum of Aviation in D.C. years ago and there was this little plaque on the wall with a picture of Bessie Coleman. I was just fascinated by the story of this woman. Who is she? How did she get to France and fly a plane when she had barely a high school education? What spirit. What courage. It seems impossible—and yet every year in Chicago to this day they fly planes and drop roses in her honor. She wanted to show black kids what was possible—that you could fly like a bird in a time when planes were a very new thing."

Angela next starred in *Supernova,* a science fiction film in which she plays Dr. Kaela Evers, who is stationed on board a medical rescue spaceship called the *Nightingale.* When the *Nightingale* and its crew receive a distress signal from deep space, they must "dimension-jump" through several galaxies in order to answer the call.

The *Nightingale* rescues a mysterious man named Karl Larson, who brings on board the ship an alien artifact that has the ability to give superhuman strength to anyone who touches it. Karl goes on a murderous rampage against the *Nightingale* crew when copilot Nick Vanzant, played by James Spader, wants to eject the object into space. Kaela and Nick try to outwit the killer, who is determined to destroy them and steal their ship.

Bassett appreciated the color-blind casting of the film: "I'm the love interest of James Spader's character. It's no thing that he's white and I'm black, but we have something to conquer. We're faced with a dilemma and we do our best to solve it. I really appreciated that [director] Walter Hill had the vision to make this different."

Unfortunately, critics didn't appreciate the predictable plot of *Supernova.* Some said it was a confusing mix of *Alien, Star Trek,* and *Twilight Zone* episodes. Kevin Thomas of the *Los Angeles Times* said the movie has "a hazy narrative line with minimal characterization. Even so, Spader and Bassett, equally assured and sharp, strike sparks and it would be fun to see them reteamed in more elevated circumstances."

In her next film, Angela and Danny Glover would reunite in *Boesman and Lena.* In 1969, Athol

Alhtough Supernova *didn't do well in theaters, Angela's performance once again challenged her audience's opinion of an acceptable role for a black actress.*

Fugard wrote *Boesman and Lena* as a stage play condemning apartheid, the policy of racial segregation and discrimination of blacks in South Africa. In 1970, John Berry staged the first New York production of the play, which featured James Earl Jones and Ruby Dee. Berry would direct Angela and Glover in the title roles for the 2000 film version.

The story takes place in Capetown, South Africa, where Boesman and Lena, a homeless couple, have been wandering since their shantytown home was bulldozed by the South African authorities. There are flashbacks to earlier times in their lives, both happy and tragic. Yet, most of the movie consists of dialogue between Boesman and Lena, in which Lena bitterly blames her husband for the suffering in their lives.

The picture was filmed on location in South Africa. Columnist Liz Smith asked Angela if she minded forsaking all vanity for the role. "No way,"

Angela told her. "I loved it. What a relief. I had to work in mud and rain and dirt. They put a scar on my face. I didn't wear makeup. It couldn't have been less glamorous or more fulfilling. As far as I'm concerned, they can film me any way they want, as long as the work is good."

Angela told *TV Guide Online* her secret for coping with the harsh filming conditions, "There was only one way to cope. On weekends you just go and get pampered physically and have them suck the dirt out of you. I'd go for a nice massage or a facial, but I'd know that the next day I was going to have to go back to the set and do it all over again."

Angela's next challenge would give her an introduction to what goes on behind the cameras, in the Showtime TV production *Ruby's Bucket of Blood*. In this story, Angela plays the owner of a Louisiana juke joint who loses her star singer and hires a white singer to fill in. Angela downplays her first producing credit. "Basically, it was me suggesting things to the director, which he accepted, a little bit to my surprise. I'm also going into the editing room and seeing how all that's done."

When asked if she's also interested in directing, Angela enthusiastically replies, "You bet. That's what I'm planning to do next. I'm looking at scripts and directing is the next step. I want the whole deal, baby!"

The whole deal for Angela also includes giving back to the community. When she's not busy working on movie projects, Angela volunteers her time and presence at many charity events. One activity especially close to her heart is the 52nd Street Project, which helps children from the Hell's Kitchen section of New York City experience all aspects of theater— though it is not your typical children's theater *Cinderella* and *Pinocchio* performing. Willie Reale, director of the program, encourages the children to come up with real-life experiences, which are then

Always the picture of strength and confidence, Angela continues to carve out a unique niche in the Hollywood community.

turned into plays with the help of professional theater people serving as coaches and mentors.

The project attracts loyal volunteers, many of whom first contributed their time when they were "unknowns" and still give of their talents now that they have become celebrities. Angela enjoys helping children become excited about acting. She remembers what it felt like to be inspired by live stage productions.

Recently, Angela completed her 21st feature film, titled *The Score*, with Robert De Niro and Marlon Brando. Not only was she the leading lady, she was, as she told Liz Smith, "the only lady. I was the love interest. And I was happy to do it because the role was written simply for a woman, not a black woman, just a woman. So, I guess we are making some progress . . . I know I'm doing my part!"

There's no doubt about that. For every role Angela Bassett plays, from sci-fi action heroines to biographical figures, she brings passion, grace, and a fiery intensity to the part. From Broadway to Hollywood, she is one of the few African-American talents to consistently break the color barrier, an achievement that is a testimony to her exceptional acting abilities. From her humble beginnings in the projects of Harlem to her successful career on stage, screen, and television, Angela has strived for excellence in her personal as well as her professional life.

When *Ebony* recently asked Angela about her phenomenal success, she simply cited the three T's—timing, talent, and tenacity. But most of all, she attributes her ability to overcome adversity to the wonderful lessons that her mother taught her growing up in St. Petersburg. "It's in my background to persevere." Angela explained. "I'm a strong black woman. My mother is a strong black woman. So are my grandmother and my great-grandmother and my aunt. If nothing else ever happened, I know that I'd keep working. And if it all went away tomorrow, I know that I'd endure."

CHRONOLOGY

1958 Angela Bassett is born on August 16, in Harlem in New York City

1962 Moves to St. Petersburg, Florida, with her mother Betty and sister D'nette

1974 Attends a performance of John Steinbeck's *Of Mice and Men* at the Kennedy Center in Washington and decides to become an actress

1976 Graduates from Boca Ciega High School, outside St. Petersburg, Florida; enrolls at Yale University in New Haven, Connecticut

1980 Graduates from Yale with a B.A. in African-American Studies; enrolls in the Yale School of Drama

1983 Graduates with a Master of Fine Arts from the Yale School of Drama and moves to New York City; lands her first role in an off-off-Broadway production of Jean Anouilh's *Antigone*; performs with the Negro Ensemble Company

1984 Appears in Broadway productions of August Wilson's plays *Ma Rainey's Black Bottom* and *Joe Turner's Come and Gone*

1988 Leaves New York for Hollywood, giving herself just six months to find success

1989 Appears in the television series *A Man Called Hawk* as Hawk's girlfriend

1991 Appears in John Singleton's *Boyz N the Hood* as the main character's mother

1992 Portrays Betty Shabazz in Spike Lee's film *Malcolm X*; portrays Katherine Jackson in the TV miniseries *The Jacksons: An American Dream*

1993 Portrays Tina Turner in *What's Love Got to Do with It?*

1995 Nominated for an Academy Award for Best Actress for *What's Love Got to Do with It?*; stars as Bernadine Harris in *Waiting to Exhale*; appears in three other movies: *Vampire in Brooklyn*, *Panther*, and *Strange Days*

1997 Marries actor Courtney B. Vance; plays Rachel Constantine in *Contact*

1998 Stars with Whoopi Goldberg in *How Stella Got Her Groove Back*

1999	Portrays principal Janet Williams in *Music of the Heart* and aviator Bessie Coleman in *Wings Against the Wind*
2000	Stars in *Supernova*; stars with Danny Glover in *Boesman and Lena*
2001	Stars with Robert De Niro and Marlon Brando in *The Score*; receives both acting and directing credits for the Showtime TV production *Ruby's Bucket of Blood*

SELECTED FILMOGRAPHY

F/X (1986)

Boyz N the Hood (1991)

City of Hope (1991)

Critters 4 (1991)

Innocent Blood (1992)

Malcolm X (1992)

Passion Fish (1992)

What's Love Got to Do with It? (1993)

Strange Days (1995)

Vampire in Brooklyn (1995)

Waiting to Exhale (1995)

Contact (1997)

How Stella Got Her Groove Back (1998)

Music of the Heart (1999)

Boesman and Lena (2000)

Supernova (2000)

The Score (2001)

Doubletake (TV movie, 1984)

The Cosby Show (TV show, 1984)

Spenser: For Hire (TV show, 1984)

227 (TV show, 1985)

Tour of Duty (TV movie, 1986)

thirtysomething (TV show, 1986)

A Man Called Hawk (TV show, 1989)

Alien Nation (TV show, 1989)

Family of Spies (TV show, 1990)

Challenger (TV movie, 1990)

The Flash (TV movie, 1990)

Perry Mason: The Case of the Silenced Singer (TV movie, 1991)

Fire: Trapped on the 37th Floor (TV movie, 1991)

In the Best Interest of the Child (TV movie, 1991)

One Special Victory (TV movie, 1991)

The Jacksons: An American Dream (TV movie, 1992)

Locked Up: A Mother's Rage (TV movie, 1992)

The Heroes of Desert Storm (TV movie, 1992)

Africans in America: America's Journey Through Slavery (TV movie, 1998)

Our Friend, Martin (TV movie, 1998)

Wings Against the Wind (TV movie, 1999)

Ruby's Bucket of Blood (TV movie, 2001)

Off the Menu: The Last Days of Chasen's (1998)

A Century of Women (TV movie, voice only, 1994)

Whispers: An Elephant's Tale (voice only, 2000)

AWARDS

———— ✿ ————

1993   NAACP Image Award: Outstanding Lead Actress in a Motion Picture, *What's Love Got to Do with It?*
Golden Globe: Best Actress in a Motion Picture (Musical or Comedy), *What's Love Got to Do with It?*
NAACP Image Award: Outstanding Supporting Actress in a Motion Picture, *Malcolm X*

1994   Oscar Nomination for Best Actress, *What's Love Got to Do with It?*

MTV Movie Award Nomination for Best Female Performance, *What's Love Got to Do with It?*
Golden Apple Award for Female Discovery of the Year

1995   National Association of Black Owned Broadcasters: Pioneer Award for Entertainer of the Year
NAACP Image Award: Outstanding Lead Actress in a Motion Picture, *Waiting to Exhale*
Women in Film: Crystal Award, *Waiting to Exhale*
Saturn Award from the Academy of Science Fiction, Horror, and Fantasy Films, *Strange Days*

1998   NAACP Image Award: Outstanding Lead Actress in a Motion Picture, *How Stella Got Her Groove Back*

2000   NAACP Image Award: Outstanding Supporting Actress in a Motion Picture, *Music of the Heart*

FURTHER READING

Books

Barr, Tony, Eric Stephen Kline, and Edward Asner. *Acting for the Camera*. New York: HarperCollins, 1997.

Collier, Aldore. "'Stella' and Angela Bassett Get Their Groove Back," *Ebony*, September 1998.

Gregory, Deborah. "Waiting to Exhale," *Essence*, December 1995.

Hunt, Gordon. *How to Audition: For TV, Movies, Commercials, Plays and Musicals*. New York: HarperCollins, 1995.

Shurtleff, Michael and Bob Fosse. *Audition*. New York: Bantam Books, 1980.

Websites

MovieClub
    http://www.movieclub.com/spotlight/bassett/bassett.html

Hollywood.com
    http://www.hollywood.com/pressroom/premieres/stella/stella.html

African Americans in the Movies
    http://www.lib.berkeley.edu/MRC/AfricanAmBib.html

INDEX

PICTURE CREDITS

page
2: Corbis
3: Corbis
10: Corbis
12: Photofest/D. Stevens
14: Photofest
16: Corbis
18: Corbis
20: Corbis
23: Corbis
24: Photofest
26: Corbis
28: Corbis
30: Corbis
32: Corbis
34: Corbis
36: Photofest

38: Photofest/D. Stevens
40: Corbis
42: Photofest/D. Stevens
43: Photofest
44: Photofest/D. Stevens
46: Corbis
49: Corbis
52: Corbis
53: Archive Photos
55: Corbis
58: Photofest
60: Publicity Still
63: Photofest
64: Photofest
66: Photofest
68: Corbis

70: Photofest/Bruce Talamon
72: Photofest/Merie W. Wallace
74: Photofest/Françoise Duhamel
76: Photofest
78: Photofest
80: Photofest
84: Photofest
85: Photofest
87: Corbis
90: Photofest
92: Corbis
94: Photofest/Stephen Vaughan
96: Photofest/Nicola Goode

Cover: AP Photo/Tina Fineberg

DAWN FITZGERALD is a freelance writer, with a B.A. from the University of Rochester and an M.A. from John Carroll University. Her articles have been published in the *Cleveland Plain Dealer*. She lives in Rocky River, Ohio, with her husband, John, and two children, Ryan and Brynn. This is her first book published by Chelsea House.